MORE ART OF CLOSING ANY DEAL

Battle Strategies to Become a Master Sales Closer and Manager

MORE ART OF CLOSING ANY DEAL

Battle Strategies to Become a Master Sales Closer and Manager

James W. Pickens
with
I. E. Mozeson

SHAPOLSKY PUBLISHERS, INC.
NEW YORK

DEDICATION/ACKNOWLEDGMENT

*I would like to take this special opportunity
to sincerely salute
all of the master sales managers
throughout the world.*

*I would also like to
thank some very wonderful people
whose love and belief made this book possible:
Dr. Jim and Evelyn Pickens, Lindsey Janell Pickens,
Boyd Billingsley, George Billingsley,
Weston Tucker, John Soderberg, Gary Morris,
Rel Shepherd, Bruce Stumbras, Peter Leveaux,
Anthony S. Kulasa, Glenn Bolech, and Farzin Ferdosi.*

The reasonable man adapts himself to the world; the unreasonable one persists in trying to adapt the world to himself. Therefore, all progress depends on the unreasonable man.

—George Bernard Shaw

You must lose a fly to catch a trout.

—George Herbert

Contents

Introduction

All of the information in this book is based on proven sales management facts and procedures that, when faithfully practiced, will get sales closers performing at their very best. The book was written to help readers become master sales closers *and* master sales managers—a courageous goal that all salespeople, and aspiring managers, should try in every way to achieve.

With my coaching and your dedication this book will transform you, a hard-working salesperson, into a highly successful master sales closer—one who takes total control over every sales situation.

It will also change the life of the potential sales manager by showing him or her how to become one of those rare *master* sales managers.

What exactly is a master sales manager? For starters, it's a sales manager who has gained the complete respect of everyone in the firm. In addition, it is someone who can get the sales team to produce optimally under all kinds of conditions and circumstances.

I disagree with those copycat books which portray a single monolithic prototype of the successful manager. Whatever your personality, there is a type of master manager that you can emulate and become. With your drive to succeed and the unique strategies presented in this book, you will experience repeated success in this fascinating profession where the sky is the limit.

To become a master sales closer and master sales manager you must begin now, and with absolute resolve. Master managers are made, not born. Let this book guide you into the sales office command center, where you can take complete control as a self-made sovereign of the sales profession.

James W. Pickens
1991

CHAPTER 1

The "Master Sales Manager": True Ruler of the Sales Profession

A master sales manager is a person who not only can lead others, but one who also shows great courage, love, and conviction when working with his colleagues. He, or she, is a total professional, no matter the time, place, or situation.

These are the essentials. For the supporting details, read on.

THE DIFFERENT TYPES OF MASTER SALES MANAGERS

There are many sales and management books on the market today; each has its own interpretation of what a successful sales manager should be like. There are books on how he should act, what he should study, how he should dress, when he should use the technical jargon for both upper and lower management, and how he should establish leadership, solve problems, and negotiate.

These books have their good points, but nearly all of them put the subject in such a high-powered microscope that readers find them ineffective and forgettable. Lost in the tangle of technical jargon, theories, and lists is the sales professional's basic purpose: influencing customers—and in the case of sales managers, leading and motivating sales closers to produce the highest volume of transactions they are capable of achieving.

3

Those books that try to mass-produce successful sales people are missing the point. Master closers and master sales managers do not come in perfectly organized and stereotyped molds. Each and every salesperson is a very independent and unique person. A master sales manager might well use unorthodox methods to get the job done in his own specialized and effective way. But he'll also be earning genuine respect and admiration from both his sales closers and the company executives at the same time.

While master sales managers conquer their sales objectives in many different, imaginative, and fascinating ways, they all have the common ability to give their sales closers a feeling of respect and warmth. It may sound too simple or overly naive, but when all of the highly technical sales management terms are taken away, the only words which correctly describe the very foundation of a master sales manager's overall, day-to-day attitude are "respect, understanding and love."

Sure, each master sales manager has his own idiosyncrasies and his own unique methods of doing things. But when all is said and done, the successful projection of the manager's respect, understanding, and love will be the key to motivated salesmen and a winning sales firm.

Perhaps you know several different styles of athletic coaches, and you know the impact of their personality on the team. Visualize the master sales manager as a professional football coach, with the sales closers making up his team. The following descriptions of master sales managers will then be more easily understood and appreciated.

The "Wall Street" Master Sales Manager

This is the master sales manager who looks like he stepped out of a fashion magazine. With his courtesy and perfect manners he gets along with everyone, from the president of the sales company to the greenest rookie closer on the front lines. The "Wall Street" master sales manager is a perfect gentleman.

He reads, studies, and listens to all the information he can find pertaining to sales and sales management. You can put him in New York City, or in Round Rock, Nevada, and he'll succeed in one way or another every single time. He knows what he is doing and has the determination to achieve his goals.

At times, especially during an important business conversation, he can be downright intimidating. His business expertise, and command of all the relevant sales facts and figures, can make a lesser colleague feel uncomfortable. At no time, however, will he purposely throw his expertise around to boost his own ego or to put someone else down.

While the "Wall Street" master sales manager takes his job and his profession very seriously, he is not too distant to empathize somewhat with his sales staff, taking into consideration their personal goals and problems.

This master sales manager has his head screwed on straight. He successfully leads his men, not only by knowing the sales business thoroughly, but also by looking the part of a successful businessman. His impeccable grooming and wardrobe reflect his brand of leadership and professionalism. He is as likely to compliment one of his closers for a smart new suit, as he is to applaud a sterling sales performance. While few people in the company feel a strong affection for this kind of manager, everyone admires and respects him: he gets results.

The "Good Old Boy" Master Sales Manager

If the "Wall Street" manager is never seen without his well-tailored suit, the "Good Old Boy" manager's sport jacket is often slung over a shoulder or on the back of a chair. Just as the name implies, everyone likes this type of master sales manager, from the company's owners to the company's janitors. They like him because this manager is kind, caring and understanding.

The "Good Old Boy" sales manager has a pure country air about him. In fact, he's a lot like an old, down-home philosopher in the way he handles different sales management situations. For example, when a sales closer has a problem, it's the "Good Old Boy" manager who is the first person to console the distressed sales closer. This kind of master manager calms the closer down and eases the emotional burden by taking on the problem himself. The manager is so involved that the sales closer's problem becomes his own.

This type of master sales manager knows professional sales almost as well as the "Wall Street" manager, but he never seems to use his knowledge as a badge. His real strong point is that he intimately knows his sales closers and how best to work with them. The "Good Old Boy" master manager cares about his closers and treats them like family. His staff returns his affection—with productivity.

The "Fear and Intimidation" Master Sales Manager

This type of master sales manager has lightning in his eyes and thunder in his voice.

Maybe that's why his office sees no storm clouds and feels no ripples on the high seas of salesmanship. At times you feel like you've got Captain Ahab at the helm, but the hold is bursting with the whale blubber of success. Some of the closers grumble and even desert ship, but the crew that stays on has an abiding respect for their manager, and a burning desire to perform at their best.

The "Fear and Intimidation" manager can be as rough and demanding as a Marine drill sergeant, but he's doing his job professionally, financially benefitting his company and his individual sales closers. This type of master sales manager exhibits a heart of cold steel, but in reality, he's got a heart of gold. He'll do anything to help out one of his sales closers who gets into trouble, but the closer had better be ready for a good old dressing down when the problem is cleared up and over.

This masterful sales manager can control and motivate hundreds of sales closers at one time. He runs a large staff meeting like a war room, with himself as commander. Then again, he can take on one individual closer and give him all of the attention and straightening out he needs to get back on the "selling" track.

This Marine drill sergeant manager wants "a few good men." He wants a lean and mean sales force, and won't hesitate to give a slacking closer his honorable discharge. Any firings will usually be discreet, without a stormy public scene. While this manager can be brutal at times, he always behaves with gentlemanly class. At a staff meeting he'll explain that a missing colleague had no longer maintained a fruitful relationship with the firm. Somehow his icy euphemism is far more effective than a lesser manager's loud ranting about why Henderson was fired. Instead of conspiratorial grumbling and sympathy resignations, the closers tend to rally around their manager with loyalty and pride. They are even a little thrilled to know that they made the grade and Henderson didn't.

The "Fear and Intimidation" manager does issue carrots as well as sticks. Getting a word of public commendation from this manager can be worth several hugs from a "Good Old Boy" manager. In his own slightly aloof way, the intimidating master sales manager shows his pride and affection for his closers, his loyal, elite guard. Making fear and intimidation work for him, this strong father figure gains the respect and admiration of his sales closers, and fosters a hunger for his approval.

In time, the closers are molded in their manager's image. They do become his loyal, professional sales team, a unique group of people that he constantly motivates and challenges to outsell any competition that his sales company faces. In fact, his team usually does just that. They most often outsell everyone else on the march to an objective goal set out by their intimidating, but inspiring, master manager.

The "Rah-Rah" Master Sales Manager

The "Rah-Rah" master sales manager will get master sales closers excited and enthusiastic about sales, customers, team goals and life itself. He is not merely "Mr. Optimism," he is more like Reverend Optimism. When everyone else feels low at an early morning sales meeting, he takes over and gets things turned around. This master sales manager's enthusiasm is infectious. It is no wonder that everyone likes to be around him. If brought into a sales division where things seem depressed, chaotic, or just plain unsuccessful, he will, more likely than all the others, get a sales force moving in the right direction.

The "Rah-Rah" manager's fire also has an effect on dull or "deadbeat" customers. When a sales closer needs help getting a sale from one of these "laid back" customers, all the closer has to do is call in the "Rah-Rah" master manager to "T. O." (take over) the sale, and then just watch this so-called "difficult" customer's reaction. The result is like a bolt of lightning. All of a sudden there is a new and powerful surge of energy at the closing table, and chances are more than good that the reserved and hesitant customer will catch the enthusiasm and purchase the product—amazing everyone in the sales office.

Like Reverend Optimism, the "Rah-Rah" master sales manager keeps the energy level turned on by complete faith in himself and his maker. His line of products is the Good News, and he wants his closers, his apostles, to be downright evangelical. A sales campaign becomes a crusade, the sales meeting his pulpit. At meetings you'll see him jump up and down, clap his hands, or even sing out loud. He can make you feel good about beating those devils at the competing dealership or corporation. Not everybody can meet his nine-to-five smiles and firm handshakes, but the bottom line is that he does his job, he gets sales. Most everyone associated with him not only makes money, but is happy and excited while doing it.

The "Negative" Master Sales Manager

Don't let this title mislead you. This type of master sales manager is a far cry from being negative in his attitude, but he does demonstrate negative approaches in his sales management. He uses a lot of reverse psychology on his sales closers. For example, at a meeting he'll tell his sales closers that they have to reach a certain goal of sales volume by the next day. Then, before closing the meeting, he'll add that he wouldn't be surprised if the closers fell short of the intended goal, that they might not have it in them to meet the challenge. He somehow gets the closers highly motivated to prove him wrong and to prove themselves.

On the personal level, he will privately tell a sales closer that he is very disappointed in his sales closing percentages. Then he'll add, like an afterthought, "I thought you were better than that, Mr. Closer, I guess I was wrong. I overestimated you." Unless the closer is a real loser, he often responds with a superlative effort to earn the raised eyebrows and affirmative nod of his manager.

These two illustrations help you see where the term "negative" comes from to describe this manipulative sales manager. One couldn't get more opposite the "Rah-Rah" manager's mode of operation. The "Negative" manager is using intimidation of a different sort—getting the closer motivated to avoid shame and prove his self-worth.

This type of master manager gets the job done and produces solid sales figures without overt methods, like threatening job security. Instead, he subtly plants "thought seeds" in a sales closer's mind. He makes the closer realize, on his own, that he really can do a much better job. The "Negative" master sales manager senses which closers would have the most productive reactions to his devious implantations. He's a regular Ph.D. of Reverse Psychology, treating his closers like patients. Most of these "patients" do get better, and the sales figures get teased, prodded and provoked to greater heights. This special master sales manager is not a very excitable person and, compared to the "Rah-Rah Manager," he barely seems to breath. But, he never gets flustered when things go wrong. Quite the contrary, he is calm, quiet and patient, always looking for a sound and fair solution to any internal problems or outside obstacles. He will always stay cool-headed, where the more emotional managers will make a bad situation worse.

When things go right for the whole sales division or for an individual closer, the "Negative" master manager will simply say nothing, nod his head in the affirmative, and display a slight smile. Somehow that small gesture from the "Negative" master manager says it all, and a closer can be charged from that small spark for weeks to come.

The "Playboy" Master Sales Manager

How this master sales manager does his job, no one knows. But he does it, and he does it well. The "Playboy" sales manager basically has a lot of fun. He motivates through pleasure as effectively as the intimidating managers do through displeasure. He enjoys his work and his play, sometimes both at the same time. But again, what can you say? The higher-ups can't complain because his sales force's performance is excellent. No matter how tired he ought to be after a weekend, or a late night escapade, he always has his business under control and in proper order.

He can't be accused of corrupting anybody with his hedonistic ways, as he is too discreet to socialize with company personnel beyond the bounds of office parties. Back at the office the "Playboy" is always exuding the cologne of charisma. His closers eagerly perform at their best to better bask in their manager's popularity and better fantasize that they could be like him.

This particular manager is a rare breed. He combines a true happy-go-lucky personality with good business sense. He can sell his products with the best of them, using little more than his charm. He knows, and uses, all the little tricks of professional sales that get contracts signed. He inspires his closers to do likewise, even though they lack his natural abilities to charm a contract onto the signing table. Some of the sales closers don't really know how to take this type of master sales manager. Maybe there's a little jealousy on such a closer's part, or he just can't figure out what makes this "Playboy" manager tick. Whatever the differences that might exist between a few of the sales closers and this unusual kind of sales manager, they don't really matter in the long run. The bottom line for everyone concerned in sales is that this "Playboy" master manager gets top sales performances from his company's closers.

The "Playboy" manages to succeed while having such a good time because his smile is real. He is genuinely happy to see his co-workers in the morning. It doesn't matter that his happiness feeds on the adoration of the staff, because there is usually plenty of cheer to go around. He sincerely does enjoy work as much as play, and he can make selling as much fun as a tennis match or a romantic conquest. Those who resent his dominant popularity get won over by his dazzling salesmanship and knowledge of the business. If "Playboy" doesn't handle the minute details as well as the "Negative" manager —it doesn't matter. There is always someone eager to help the "Playboy" out. Because things are usually in such good shape, he can afford to take that extra morning off to play golf with the big brass or leave early to go wining and dining with major clients.

While some of his detractors feel that his mind isn't on business, the "Playboy" surprises people by reading up on professional sales and sales management. He is a true sales pro, who fully accepts his responsibilities to his closers and to his company.

Just let sales fall off and—surprise! This master manager will suddenly appear from nowhere with enough force and fire to get things squared away fast! As much as he loves a good time, the "Playboy" master sales manager loves making a lot of money—not only for himself, but for his sales closers as well. Who better than this manager gets the message across that good selling will pay for good times?

The "By-the-Book" Master Sales Manager

This master manager couldn't be more different than the "Playboy" manager. He doesn't seem to know how to have, or give, any pleasure—except when it comes to payday. The "By-the-Book" manager doesn't often crack a smile, so the loyalty between closer and manager tends to be purely financial.

This regimented master sales manager is a company man. While the sales closers that work with him accomplish their career objectives to the maximum, the manager's strong company allegiance dampens any real friendship or loyalty between himself and the sales staff. The closers have a great deal of respect for this manager, and that is the chemistry that allows the "By-the-Book" manager to excel.

This master manager gets along best with the truly professional closers who can appreciate his quiet competence. The "By-the-Book" manager lives up to all his responsibilities to his sales force and to his sales company. No other master manager beats him at that. As smart as he is in the business sense, however, he falls short when it comes to interpersonal relations or "people sense."

This kind of master manager is sometimes resented for being too much of a company man, but he'll always try to be fair when dealing with his sales closers. When a sales closer approaches this manager in a time of real need, this company-oriented manager will usually pull through for the sales closer. His heart isn't entirely locked up in the company safe.

The sales closers maintain respect for this master manager, who, whether right or wrong in his assessment of a problem, will always show instantaneous and firm conviction in his decisions. Even if he's too consistent for some tastes, he will always take a stand on an issue and never allow a problem to fester in a series of inconclusive staff meetings. His predictability is dull to some, but very comforting to others.

An endangered species in the industry, these "By-the-Book" master managers are much appreciated by the more conservative closers who don't mind sticking to the rules of the selling game. Closers who feel that company rules are made to be bent or broken had better check the "Help Wanted" ads before they find themselves in the predicament of looking for a job while out of one.

These managers are not easy to work with and are nearly impossible to befriend. Closers who can put up with this master manager's all-work-and-no-play attitude can thrive professionally. This manager tends to develop a loyal core of closers, even though the employees share none of the emotional intensity of some of the other managers' troopers or apostles. It's no secret that some better marriages don't work on love.

The "Teacher" Master Sales Manager

Any sales closer would be fortunate to find himself on this type of manager's sales force. The "Teacher" master sales manager is one of the very best. Not only is he great at his job, but he also enjoys sharing his professional sales knowledge with others. He is a master instructor who will always take the time to sit down with any sales closer and explain in detail the tactics of closing sales and knowing customers. This unselfish type of sales manager is not jealous of others' success. Unlike the partisan "Fear and Intimidation" manager, he can be happy for the success of an innovative sales campaign at a rival company or division. He's as hungry for new sales techniques as the "By-the-Book" manager is wary of them.

The "Teacher" master manager keeps the everyday flow of new sales information circulating around the sales office so that other managers and their sales closers can learn and grow, thus bettering not only the firm, but the entire sales profession. He's the ideal teacher to break in a new closer because he is an eternal student in the field. He completely understands sales closers because he remains one himself. The "Teacher" energetically helps a sales closer with professional or personal problems. He feels it is part of his job, while the "Playboy" or "By-the-Book" manager considers coaching or counseling to be a waste of valuable time. The "Teacher" master manager can usually teach from years of experience, as well as sharing the latest trends. The "Teacher" would be one of the top sales closers anywhere if he were to return to the sales force; he is not one of those who manage because he can not do it himself.

This kind of master sales manager is hard to find. There is not a sales force anywhere in the world that would not want to have this type of master manager on board. And there is no sales closer anywhere who wouldn't gain valuable insights by listening to and taking notes from this talented master manager. This doesn't mean that every closer likes the "Teacher" manager. A few very private types might actually resent this manager as a busybody. Perhaps they need the more intense emotional support offered by some of the other master managers discussed above. To the majority of professional closers, however, the bonds with the "Teacher" manager are those of gratitude. These closers are thankful that this manager is so often, and so skillfully, minding their business.

The "Positive" Master Sales Manager

This master sales manager differs from the "Rah-Rah" manager mentioned above. True, the "Positive" master sales manager always has a good, healthy outlook on business and life, but he demonstrates this in a quiet manner. This kind of master manager won't be found running around the sales office patting all the sales closers on the back, jumping up and down at a sales meeting, or otherwise getting everyone's adrenalin flowing. That's not his style. In fact, he's more like the mirror opposite of the "Negative" manager. He'll look a closer in the eye and say, "I know you can do it." Instead of motivating with reverse psychology, the "Positive" manager motivates with a slow, steady "can do" attitude that allows tortoises to beat hares even in the world of sales.

This type of master sales manager will, at his own pace, quietly walk around the sales office with a pleasant smile on his face, interested in the good of everyone. He takes the time to listen to anyone's problems and will do all he can to help. He works wonders with unhappy customers and can give a depressed sales closer a ray of redemptive sunshine along with a few quiet words of encouragement. If a closer is slumping, this manager will stress the best thing about that closer or his performance, giving him praise when he needs it most. The "Positive" master sales manager is an asset to the sales team because he turns any troubling situation into a challenge that can, and will, be overcome.

Instead of playing his closers against each other to increase productivity through competition, the "Positive" manager tries to keep his closers working together harmoniously. He has an eye for spotting and diffusing trouble between closers. While he is too low-key for some, this manager wins over most of the staff by combining some of the affection of the "Good Old Boy" manager with some of the guidance of the "Teacher" manager. Most closers will do anything to keep working for the "Positive" sales manager because they want to soak in his calmness, stability and optimism for the world beyond the sales office as well.

The master sales managers outlined above will give the reader a good idea of the many different and interesting personalities that make up this highly specialized profession. It should always be remembered that the master sales manager, no matter what kind of unique personality he has, is the very backbone of any sales organization. Without this strong, charismatic or pace-setting leader the sales closers, no matter how good they are, would not be as organized, productive, or rich on commissions. The master manager is blessed with a good measure of courage, love or conviction and uses these gifts in his own special way to lead men and women down the path of success.

THE "SIDEKICK" SALES MANAGER: THE MASTER SALES MANAGER'S PROFESSIONAL PARTNER

Few master sales managers can function well without a competent partner, "Sidekick," or right-hand man. The sales closers have many nicknames for this managerial second-in-command, and most of them—"flunky," "go-for," "yes man"—are not as friendly as "Sidekick." Whatever the closers call him really doesn't matter, as the "Sidekick" manager has a very important function within the overall sales organization. Without this "Sidekick," or trusted ally, the head honcho, or number one manager, would be at a severe loss.

More than an understudy bucking for promotion, the best "Sidekick" encourages and supports the manager. The assistant manager must carry out directives dependably and step in capably to take the helm when necessary. No matter how strong a personality he is, the "Sidekick" must submerge any dominance to harmonize with the boss. Just as the president of a company has to have his vice president and a talk-show host has to have his co-host. Every good marriage, too, needs one partner who can graciously compromise and let the spouse lead in his or her area of strength.

In too many cases the "Sidekicks" are mediocre managers who do not learn enough about leadership from the master managers they work with. Ideally, the "Sidekick" must consider himself the head of the sales force, but with one man above him. In the chain of command he is the first lieutenant and the manager is the captain. In the best of armies and sales forces the men don't miss a beat when the commander is out of action. Especially if the manager's absence is temporary, the competent "Sidekick" should try to maintain the same pace and tone of work so that productivity doesn't lag in the confusion of a different tempo. Only if the "Sidekick" is being kicked upstairs to the top spot, should he gradually change the mode of operation to suit his own style.

The sales force differs from the army in that there is no Officers Club to isolate the assistant manager (first lieutenant) from the closers (enlisted men). The "Sidekick" is free to circulate among the sales people and to check up on problems between the manager and the closers. It is his job to solve or mediate those problems before they get big enough to disrupt the work flow. The best assistant managers can smooth things out without appearing to favor the boss or the closers. When the "Sidekick" manager does take sides, he will nearly always be in the sales manager's corner. (He has to be, if he wants to keep his job.)

The "Sidekick" manager can still enjoy freedom of movement within the sales force if he doesn't get himself pegged as the boss's lackey. He must show some empathy for the closer with a grievance, even if he thinks the employee is in the wrong. The "Sidekick" must make it clear that he is not the sales manager, and that he does not have the final word. This will prevent a sales closer from getting upset with the assistant manager when discussing the problem at hand. The closers should feel that the "Sidekick" manager is their reliable ally to pass their complaints or arguments along to the sales manager. It takes some doing for the assistant manager to convince both the manager and the closers that he is a reliable advocate for their side in a dispute, but these are the kinds of skills that will keep him at number two until the top spot is open.

The professional "Sidekick" manager should know the full sales office routine and all the responsibilities that have to be performed to run an efficient sales force. For instance, the assistant manager is the one who takes roll call at the sales meetings. He is the audience warm-up man for the sales manager's morning sales talk, and he ought to know enough about the topic to give some intelligent background material. He is the one who makes sure that all the sales contracts are signed properly and that the paperwork is in order. If the support staff and secretarial pool do not have their own designated leader, the "Sidekick" has to play office manager as well.

The assistant manager is the one who has to listen to all of the sales manager's gripes, war stories and bad jokes. He has to put up with the boss's emotional needs as well as his business requirements. It could be harrowing to play second fiddle to the "Fear and Intimidation" master manager, and it might be fun to be a satellite of the "Playboy" manager. Of course the closers, too, come in a wide assortment and have the most incredible talent for getting into strange predicaments. Personality conflicts develop between closers as well, and this first lieutenant can't just call in the M.P.s. He'll have to settle the problems himself and get things back in good working order, along with a positive team spirit.

The "Sidekick" sales manager will always have one very important job requirement that is never discussed openly and will never appear on a job description. He should protect and watch out for the sales manager's blind side, guarding the managers back from any derogatory statements or negative opinions that might circulate from within the sales force or company. These harsh statements or vicious rumors may have sprung from petty rivalries or serious incidents, but they could undermine the effectiveness of the manager and hurt sales production. The "Sidekick" manager must never think that a wave of discontent or scandal will carry him to the top. In many dismissals, the assistant coaches go out with the head coach.

As well as being the manager's chief of intelligence, the number two person has to be alert for any developments that come between the hierarchy and his direct boss. The timely execution of some "tiptoe" diplomacy might cover up for the sales manager when careers are on the line. The job you save might be your own.

As one can see, the "Sidekick" manager has many important functions that help keep the ball rolling. He is much more than a nursemaid, peacekeeper, and friend to the sales closers and the sales manager. He is the person who keeps the sales force together, so that the sales closers can do the job that they know best (selling), and the sales manager can do the job he knows best (guiding the sales closers).

Now, the assistant manager comes in as many varieties as the master manager himself. Let us explore three major kinds of "Sidekicks" who have attained the level of master managers in their own right:

a. The "Positive Sidekick"

b. The "Negative Sidekick"

c. The "Yes-Man Sidekick"

The "Positive Sidekick" Manager

This "Sidekick" lights up the sales office with enthusiasm. He loves his work and does not feel apprehensive about his position or his prospects of rising up to the managerial seat. His contentment puts the closers, and even the customers, at ease; the manager is confident in his public relations abilities. This "Sidekick" manager may be more talented than his boss, but he never lets on that he deserves the top spot. When his initiative is needed, he'll gently prod the manager along with charm and good timing, so that the boss is unaware that his assistant is calling the shots. Just as this "Sidekick" knows how much he and the boss can push individual closers, the "Positive" assistant manager knows just how far the manager can be pushed.

The "Positive Sidekick" manager has no enemies. The sales closers feel that he is their friend and advocate in any difficulties with the boss. He works to maintain harmony between the closers and management, and between the closers themselves. The "Positive Sidekick" wants only to keep the closers geared up for sales, with no energy frittered on "negative" squabbling. This type of assistant manager puts both his boss and those below him at ease with his "everything will be okay" personality; his style makes him a valuable asset to the firm.

The "Negative Sidekick" Sales Manager

On the surface, it looks like this kind of "Sidekick" manager dislikes his job, the closers, and even the customers. This "Negative" assistant manager usually has an emphatic "No!" for sales closers who want to try a new sales approach or who need help with their personal finances. All this negativism is his way of setting up an intimidating front that gives him a smooth run with his subordinates. When the closers finally do get that affirmative response, or positive comment, they become high with unexpected approval—like a starving man getting thrown a steak. Keeping his closers psychologically hungry keeps them financially well fed, working and earning their maximum.

This "Negative Sidekick" manager is a natural at what he does. It would be disastrous for another to attempt to imitate his method and style. This kind of masterly assistant manager not only wins the begrudging loyalty of his closers, but is appreciated and respected by his superior as well. This "Sidekick's" manager could not be the "Positive" or "Rah-Rah" types previously discussed. Instead, he needs to work with either a subdued management style or one that does not clash with his own.

The "Yes-Man Sidekick" Manager

Just as the name implies, he's the sales manager's biggest ego booster.

The "Yes-Man Sidekick" is more than just a competent executor of the manager's orders, he is a skilled doer as well. He knows selling well enough to "T.O." (take over) for sales closers. He also knows sales contracts and sales paperwork inside and out, and doesn't have to bother his superiors with procedural matters. He works long hours and is on twenty-four hour call. Nonetheless, he has the energy and the loyalty to always back up the sales manager when necessary.

It sounds as if this type of "Sidekick" manager is, in fact, a master sales manager on his own accord. This is true, but for now this "partner" or "number two" management position is exactly what he wants at this particular stage in his life. He gets satisfaction out of being a superb "Yes-Man." When a higher position calls, he might just step up, or step out to another firm. In the meantime, he cheerfully keeps in step.

If he has any flaws, the "Yes-Man Sidekick" manager may have to work on being a more likable person. He helps his sales closers and will go out of his way to help customers, but one can't get around the irritating fact that he is always in complete agreement with everything his boss, the sales manager, has to say. No matter what the sales manager is discussing, whether it's sales, politics, sports or stale jokes, the "Yes-Man" will most always second his manager's motions or viewpoints.

It might also get on the closers' nerves that the "Yes-Man Sidekick" prefers the boss company on anything from fishing trips to formal dinner parties. Behind the "Yes-Man's" back the closers sneer that the assistant manager drives the same car and wears the same suits as the manager to curry favor with the boss. This servile tendency to mirror the manager cuts into the staff's respect for the "Yes-Man Sidekick."

Ironically, the major motivation for this "Sidekick's" imitation of his boss is that deep down he wants to be liked and respected by the sales closers, in the same way that they like and respect their manager. As the "Yes-Man" grows into a top managerial position of his own, he will likely see that he can gain full respect for being who he is, and not for whom he'd like to be. Even before he evolves into a master manager on his own right, this type of "Sidekick" sales manager wins more admiration than he knows for doing a great job for his sales organization.

Even the most unique and charismatic master managers have spent a similar period apprenticing as a wormy "Yes-Man." Just look at the world of professional sports. Most of the dominant head coaches in the National Football League today were assistant coaches, following someone else's orders just a few seasons ago. You see, being a "Yes-Man" is not an incurable disease. However, it can be a career-long affliction for someone who only feels confident in the shadow of a dominant leader.

THE SPECIAL "MAKEUP" OF A MASTER SALES MANAGER
The Leadership Principle

There are as many ways to become a master sales manager as there are people with different qualities who want to become professional sales managers. The only common denominator is excellence and that special "self-igniting leadership element." All of the profiles of master managers include the ability to motivate and encourage oneself, and therefore to reach out to others.

This special ability enables the potential master sales manager to be a step ahead of the crowd when it comes to reaching goals and meeting responsibilities. This "self-igniting leadership element" can also be described as a powerful inner belief in oneself, a faith so tangible that the individual inspires others to believe in him.

One's character must innately contain a spark of this "self-igniting leadership element" as there are no textbook skills in the world that will compensate if one wants to become a master sales manager, rather than a mildly competent one. It is hoped that readers can find their path to management mastery within this book, and learn to fan their inner sparks of ambition into this "self-igniting" flame that can transform you into a torch bearer.

(See Chapter 3, "Preparing the Sales Team," for more details on how one can achieve and utilize this magical "self-igniting leadership element.") On the way to achieving sales mastery it is very important to note the personal and educational background of a master sales manager.

The Master Sales Manager's Background

There is no M.B.A. or other formal educational requirement needed to become a professional master sales manager. The best "degrees" are won in the School of Hard Knocks. (Knocks on the door-to-door route or cold calling on the phone will earn a rookie salesman quite a few credits in that School of Hard Knocks.)

Every master sales manager has his own unique story to tell in regard to his background and/or education. For instance, some master sales managers have never finished high school, while there are others who hold doctoral degrees from the finest colleges and universities in the world. (Those degrees are not necessarily in business.) Some master sales managers come from stable, and even wealthy, families, while others come from broken homes, with no money at all. The calm of one's background might lead one to be a "Wall Street" master manager, while the pain and emotional deprivation of a contrary personal history might propel another to become a "Fear and Intimidation" master manager.

Qualitative variations in background don't really make that much difference in the long run. Manners, etiquette, poise and sophistication can be learned by the most underprivileged person. All one needs is that spark of enthusiasm and the motivation to learn from books or the skill to imitate successful people.

It must be remembered, though, that no matter what one's background or education has been, the person who does turn into a true master sales manager has to have two extra ingredients that are not fully attainable through education. These key ingredients are: *(1) belief in oneself, and (2) that wonderful, uncompromising word called courage.*

> NOTE: *There is no right age for a sales manager. He could be a child prodigy of twenty-five or a patriarch of seventy-five. It really doesn't matter, just as long as he knows his responsibilities to his sales force and can carry them out professionally.*

A young man with exceptional poise can have the "self-igniting leadership elements" of self-confidence, self-motivation and faith. The older man may have developed those traits over a forty-year period in the business. The gleam in his eye and the cadence of his voice still says "go get em" to his closers, even if his handshake isn't as firm as it used to be.

> NOTE: *You can't run a winning sales team by waving your resume and describing your past successes. You might impress the personnel office, but the closers want to know what you've done for them lately, and what you WILL do for them. Closers can tell immediately if a new sales manager is a winner or loser.*

All the fire-like imagery of a master sales manager's "self-igniting" leadership is no accident. One can light a hundred torches from a single flame, without losing any original fire. So it is that with that special motivating fire of a master manager, his flaming enthusiasm spreads throughout the office until it is hot with his glow. The glow of a successful team of sales closers reflects back on the manager, fuelling him in return. Master sales managers know for a fact that what you give out is exactly what you'll get back.

For a master manager, belief in others is equally as important as belief in oneself. Even the "Negative" master manager can project to the closers that deep down he knows they can do it. Belief in oneself without the ability to kindle like feeling among the staff will only be interpreted as arrogance. No background in the world will save a manager who comes off as self-centered rather than team-centered. If a master manager has arrogance it is an outward one that says WE are the best.

Common Sense and the Master Sales Manager

Master sales managers are not only intelligent when it comes to business and sales situations, they also possess a great deal of good, old-fashioned common sense. Without this "horse sense" going for the master manager day in and day out, there is not a sales force or sales organization anywhere that wouldn't eventually self-destruct.

The master sales manager has incidents that come up every day that cannot be solved by looking up the solution in some professional guide book. Many such problems have to do with sales closers and their talent for getting into awkward predicaments. The sales manager has the responsibility of getting the problems squared away, and it is a master manager who succeeds by using his common sense. If a closer is coming to work high on drugs or alcohol, the manager with common sense will figure out the best move without resorting to an instant emotional response (such as an immediate firing) or an overly deliberate approach based on some pop psychologist's "expert" advice.

The true master manager will measure up the situation for everyone's best concern. If Walter Whiskey or Catherine Cocaine has never produced for the company and is in a position to embarrass the firm in his or her present condition then common sense would dictate a discreet but swift dismissal. If Wally or Cathy has given some fine years of service to the company, then the master manager must do what he can to retain the closer's services. Here the manager has to rely on his knowledge of the individual closer.

If they're the kind of person who can take it, the master manager will ask them about their problem in the privacy of his office. The manager will show empathy on one hand but firmness on the other. A probation period, or extended leave, will be set for the closer to get clean. Common sense tells the master manager not to mention permanent dismissal, as this talented closer can turn around and utilize those abilities for his competitor.

If Walter or Catherine could never survive an honest confrontation without quitting, the manager with common sense will have to improvise. The master manager will send a memo to his troubled closer to the effect that their two week paid vacation has been moved up to the very next day. In addition, two weeks of unpaid vacation has been added on. No drugs or alcohol are mentioned, but the closer who reads, "We value your work and look forward to seeing you four weeks hence looking and feeling like your old self again," will get the message loud and clear. Common sense now provides the closer with a "vacation" memo to save face, and not feel too chastised to return after wrestling with his demons.

Common sense is not only a tool but a special gift that all master sales managers enjoy. The master manager uses this special gift for difficult situations, like the one above, in the same way that a philosopher uses logic. A master of common sense will:

> a. Analyze the problem
> b. Weigh the alternatives
> c. Come up with a sound
>   solution that best satisfies
>   all parties involved

Like the other qualities the master managers possess, common sense cannot be automatically learned in some classroom. It has to be acquired gradually in the experiences of everyday living. An assistant manager that wants to develop more common sense ought to study the actions and thought processes of master managers. *You might want to record actual sales problems and their solutions. Your notations can form a troubleshooting guide to dealing with similar problems when you are in a managerial position.*

A sales manager comes face-to-face with new and challenging problems every day, including personnel trouble and business difficulties. The only way he is going to come out on top is by clearing out emotional reactions, checking with his instincts, and employing his innate common sense. If a sales manager has to constantly look up answers, ask higher-ups for advice or have meetings with his assistants, then he had better get a new job. The one he has now is driving him to an early death.

If you've been a happy, productive "Sidekick" manager and can't find the "horse sense" to pull the wagon on your own—give it up. The common sense of a master manager doesn't come with the new office or better paycheck. Swallow your pride and tell the company to hire a new manager; tell them that you are happier and more productive in the number two role. The courage to make important decisions on the spot is the hallmark of a master manager. It is also courageous for an assistant manager to admit when he is not ready for greater responsibilities.

In discussing a master sales manager's characteristics and behavioral patterns, it should be remembered that, with all his powers of inspiration, common sense and courage, he is but a human being. He has the same headaches and heartaches, the identical emotional and physical aches and pains as everyone else. The great difference between the master sales manager and other people in or out of the sales office is how he handles his everyday problems.

Self-Confidence and the Master Sales Manager

The self-confidence of a master sales manager really stands out. The master manager thinks and acts differently from other folks, because he is a genuine leader and problem solver. For example, if he has to fly to an important meeting and the airline he's booked on goes on strike—he refuses to be grounded. If all the other airlines are booked solid he will not just stand around like everybody else waiting on standby for a chance cancellation. He will get over to another airport and get a flight from there, or he might even rent a private plane, if his company still comes out ahead.

The master sales manager doesn't lose because he doesn't have the word in his vocabulary. His take-charge personality is also manifest in areas that don't involve problem solving. The boss might have come from a department store where small trees in planters were on sale. He gets it into his head that a half dozen trees is exactly what the sales office needs, and sure enough, they are delivered that very afternoon. The president of the company not only condones the manager's impulse purchase, but he likes the "new" office and will swear months later that those trees are responsible for the latest upswing in sales figures. The master sales manager has the calculating mind of a determined entrepreneur, yet the intuitive genius of an artist. He combines his self-confidence with a willingness to take risks; he bets on those he trusts with a prudent sense of knowing when to quit and cut his losses. (A good general knows when to retreat.) These paradoxical qualities of positive thinking and practicality, combined with courageous, but empathetic, leadership, make the master manager a unique breed.

NOTE: *Very often a master sales manager's physical appearance will reflect these characteristics of determination, self-assuredness and kindness. He walks with a leader's confidence; he stands straight with a posture of conviction; his eyes twinkle with a genuine consideration for others. Line up a master manager with a group of commuters, and he'll stick out just like a two-star general in an office full of businessmen.*

It can be pretty well guaranteed that the general, and the master manager, will stand out above the crowd, without their attire revealing their profession.

THE BEHAVIOR OF A MASTER SALES MANAGER

The Master Sales Manager in Private Life

The master sales manager tends to be a little too strict and demanding when it comes to his wife and family. In other words, he's not the easiest person to live with. The master sales manager has a habit of bringing his work, and too often his troubles, home with him. This practice doesn't help his relationship with his loved ones at all. Now this is not a wholesale condemnation, but rather an observed generalization. Of course, an exceptional master sales manager can be an ideal husband, father, wife, or mother; but there is a propensity for shedding the mastery management skills upon opening the front door of the home.

The master sales manager would like his family to run as smoothly as he runs his sales office. With expectations of ideal behavior from a spouse and children, with a minimum of contribution on the master sales manager's part, is it any wonder why resentment often builds up on both sides? It is hard for the family to understand that the master sales manager eats, sleeps and breathes his professional sales position. It is practically impossible to get him to file away all of his "sales emotions" and business thoughts the minute he walks into his own home. He is a master at masking emotions that would harm his relationship with clients, closers or owners, but when his tie comes off at home he is liable to unload those stored negative emotions and frustrations—sometimes aiming for the heart of someone he loves.

Of course taking one's business home is not just a description of emotional and psychological baggage. Many a master sales manager's personal time is disrupted by the ever-present problems of the assistant manager or one of the closers. Even if the phone is taken off the hook, the master manager may be taking home an important report to read for the next day's sales meeting, just when Junior needs help on some algebra homework or the in-laws were in the neighborhood and decided to drop in for a visit.

At home, this ever-cool and diplomatic professional might be susceptible to irritability and emotional outbursts. Well, a master manager is human, and there must be some place where he no longer behaves like a superhuman leader of men. Things will go a lot smoother if the family of the sales manager can realize how much tension and anxiety has been bottled up in the sales office all day long. A master sales manager really needs his or her family to lend positive support, understanding and lots of love. The family must realize that a master manager has been giving out a great deal of energy, consideration and love to others during his working day. The manager's only source great enough to replenish that emotion, that sincere love, is his family and his Maker.

The Master Sales Manager's Social Life

When the master sales manager attends a social function or public gathering, whether or not it's for his sales company, he appears a different person altogether. In general, he seems more relaxed and low-keyed in this setting than at the sales office or even in his own home.

There are several reasons for this changed behavior. First of all, when the master sales manager is out socially, he can wear the badge of leadership without being weighted down by its responsibilities. He can relax and forget about figures and performances even if the function is a sales party attended by the whole sales force. Instead of projecting leadership or even intimidation (in the case of the "Fear and Intimidation" manager), he can regally bask in the glory, like a well-fed lion.

While mingling congenially with the crowd, and truly enjoying himself, even the "Playboy" master sales manager will always be in control of himself. A master manager won't let alcohol or anything else get the better of him. A female master manager won't begin to flirt, or otherwise jeopardize her professional aura, and a male won't let some friendly enthusiasm loosen his tongue with foul language. Master sales managers are wary of those jealous people in the sales company who are constantly watching and waiting for them to make a spectacle of themselves. Unfortunately, there are often envious vultures circling overhead in the hope that they can swoop down on a sales manager that makes a mistake.

Furthermore, the master sales manager does not forget that he is a major representative of his sales organization, and that he is in the spotlight for all to see. The master manager will always put his best foot forward when in public and be a perfect gentleman/lady. In most any kind of social or public gathering, the master sales manager will affably work a crowd like a politician running for office. It is also interesting to note how diplomatic and noncommittal the otherwise strong-minded master manager can be at these social events, especially with people outside his sales force.

The Master Sales Manager on His Own

This fascinating species, the master sales manager, is also worth studying in those special moments of solitude. A master manager has a high level of energy, and can rarely be found lolling around on a backyard hammock. If he is, chances are he's got a management report or other serious reading in his hands. No one-track grind, the master manager is likely to keep up on current events as well as pursuing a hobby seriously.

Most master sales managers actually like to be alone. They need those quiet times to think, and keep everything in their active life in proper perspective. A master manager tends to enjoy solitary walks or fishing trips, respecting the peacefulness and organization of nature.

The master sales manager is not lonely when alone because he not only believes in himself, he likes himself. His self-confidence even allows him to laugh at himself when he makes everyday mistakes. The master sales manager seeks solitude—not to regain sanity, but to find the strength to go on being a dynamo. It might surprise the closers to see their manager at a house of worship or in deep meditation, but he has a need to get in touch with a source of wisdom and vigor beyond himself.

FIFTEEN IMPORTANT AIMS FOR A MASTER SALES MANAGER TO REMEMBER

To conclude this chapter that defines, classifies and gives background on the master sales manager, let us review some of the fifteen most important points to keep in mind:

1. No true master sales manager is afraid to make a decision or to act. He is ready to face the consequences of any mistake, taking the full responsibility upon himself. He will not blame his mistakes on someone else.
2. A master sales manager will always show courtesy to everyone he meets, no matter how bad he might feel emotionally or physically. There is never a closer or customer so infuriating that the master sales manager will blow up and lose his cool in a confrontation.
3. The master sales manager will know everything about professional sales from top to bottom. The master manager can "T.O." (take over), write up sales contracts, file, and even show an office employee how to change the ribbon on his or her computer printer.
4. The master sales manager always remembers that he is much more than just a boss to his sales closers. He is a combination of friend, father, teacher, and leader. He is always there to lend a hand.
5. A master sales manager takes it as a compliment, rather

than an insult, when one of his own sales closers accepts a managerial position at another company. It is also a supreme flattery to discover that said closer is copying the leadership mode of his old master sales manager.

6. A true master sales manager will not envy or feel resentful toward another master manager's successful sales production. Rather than displaying such insecurity, he might be spurred on to a more intense, but still friendly, rivalry.

7. A true master sales manager lives every day to the fullest, always looking at problems as challenges and their solutions as his reward. He carries this positive enthusiasm with him into every difficult situation he faces. His closers never see him perplexed or defeated by hitches or lows in business.

8. If the manager has had a rough time at home, such as a quarrel with his other half, he will not bring any edginess back to the sales office. No large, or small, outside crisis will affect his own performance or the overall sales production. The closers never see their manager looking irritable or depressed.

9. A master sales manager will always measure success by the bottom line—the closing percentages and the sales volume that his sales force produces.

10. A master manager will always keep a closer's personal problem confidential. Only with the most severe problems should the manager risk breaking the bond of trust between him and his sales force.

11. The master sales manager will be the first to encourage a sales closer when he's down, the first to congratulate a closer when he does a great job, and the first to kick some rear end when a sales closer has gotten out of line.

12. The master sales manager, even if he thinks he knows it all, will always listen attentively to the suggestions of the sales closers, the office personnel and even the janitor. His authority will never get in the way of his accessibility and empathy.

13. The master sales manager will never humiliate or criticize a sales closer in public. The entire force, including himself, can

be castigated at meetings, but individuals will never be called on the carpet. Firings and serious warnings should be executed behind closed doors.

14. The master sales manager should always take the time to listen to a sales closer's personal problems. Whether the problem seems insignificant or, on the contrary, suited for a doctor or psychoanalyst, the master manager will respect his employee's need to unburden himself to him. The master manager should foster a fatherly image, realizing that he will have to play father confessor to some, and "best pal" or daddy to others.

15. Every master sales manager should dress according to the dignity of his position, wearing a fine business suit to work and a smart golfing outfit out on the links. Even if the "Good Old Boy" manager likes to get into shirt sleeves and roll them up, let him arrive in a two-piece suit. The master sales manager not only has to have class, he has to demonstrate it.

With all the information in this chapter profiling the master sales manager, keep in mind that anyone with some basic, innate gifts, and the dedication to work on self-improvement can grow into a master sales manager as well.

CHAPTER 2

Starting Up:
The Master Sales Manager
Sets Up His Sales Office
and Sales Team

I f you are getting in to a sales firm on the ground floor, make sure your sales office is on the street level. Locate the sales office in a convenient, high-traffic neighborhood and in a location with easy access to the rest of the complex's facilities.

If you have inherited the sales office, put your signature on it with changes for the better. Make sure the office has good visual appeal, and an inviting atmosphere. Look into plants and colorful foliage arrangements to reduce the harsh steel of most office furniture. If you are not competent at interior decorating, invest in a professional.

Remember, the outside, and then the inside, of a sales office is the first thing that a customer sees. Your business should convey warmth, a family environment, and professionalism all in one visual statement.

THE SALES OFFICE
DRESSED FOR SUCCESS

Sales Office Furniture

Inside the sales office, the furniture should reflect the same kind of solid confidence exuded by a major bank. No imitation wood grain desks, folding chairs or trendy art work. The office should

35

look as though it will be there a hundred years from now. It should give the customer the feeling of a secure and respectable institution. The furnishings of a sales office give the same impression as a businessman's suit.

A customer who feels comfortable, dignified and somewhat pampered is easier for the salespeople to close. If your line of products has a showroom, don't make the mistake of having a beautiful showroom and then a makeshift office. Don't feel that the customer is already "sold" by the time he's at your desk to sign papers. Even if the client enters favorably inclined, the size of his order may plummet if he is dismayed by a tacky sales environment.

This only makes the closer's job of selling that much easier. Every single detail that helps calm the customer, gives confidence to the customer, and shows respect for the customer, will only increase sales. The sales office that utilizes this information will keep far ahead of any of its competitors.

Background Music

Every environmental detail that gives calm and confidence to the customer is worth consideration, including background music. Set up some professionally programmed background music to play throughout the entire sales office, music that will stimulate positive subconscious emotions. A professional music company will expertly select and program the kinds of music best suited for your customers.

"Oversized" Design

In some major sales offices, the sales company will purposely place oversized furniture in the reception area. This makes the customer feel physically smaller compared to the "bigness" of the furniture. This feeling works on the customer's subconscious mind by making his actions and thoughts less aggressive, bold, and egotistical. The "bigness" of the furniture overpowers the customer, and puts him in a more "humble" and "respectful" mood. This oversized furniture tactic does work, but it must complement the sales office's architecture to look natural.

Sales Office Colors

Colors are very important for a sales office, for the exterior as well as the interior. Never use a "bright red;" it only makes most customers more cautious. Colors that will positively affect people's moods include confident colors like royal blue, forest green, gold, and rich browns. There are also light, upbeat combinations that work, such as cool pastels and desert theme colors. Colors definitely affect customers' moods, and a master sales manager would do well to get professional advice in choosing the right colors for his office.

Refreshment Area

Have a special location in the sales office for refreshments. If nothing else, at least make sure that there is always fresh coffee available for the customers. This little courtesy is very important. It allows you to show hospitality and consideration for the customer. Remember, every positive step that helps relax and loosen up the customer before, and during, his meeting with the closer, helps get the customer in a purchasing frame of mind. Sales are the bottom line, and the master sales manager has to enlist every possible selling strategy to be successful.

Sales Office Technology

In the sales office, the master sales manager has to equip his office with much of the same technology used by larger corporations. The "big four" features ought to be standard:

a. *Computers*
b. *Copiers*
c. *Advanced phone system*
d. *Facsimile machine*

The reasons should be obvious, as no sales outfit can afford to lose sales because they are technologically back in the 1970s. Those old rows of files are not only unsightly and expensive—you must hire file clerks or distract your secretarial staff to obtain file information—even though you'll never pull a file fast enough to answer your customer's question, without a PC. Does the sales manager himself have to be a computer programmer? No, but a master manager ought to be computer literate enough to store and recall data himself, so as not be shown up by closers, assistant managers or office managers. In addition, many important forms can be retrieved and printed on the spot with a computer.

A copier can likewise produce needed forms, eliminating messy carbon copies and other anachronisms. Whether it's a copy of a customer's check, a contract, a sales closer's call information, or a travel record, you want to have copying capabilities under your thumb—not off in another department or tucked away in a mail room.

Beyond an answering machine to courteously and reliably take messages from customers and closers after hours, make sure you have a phone system that never gives a caller a busy signal. That caller could be going to the next number on his list and giving your competitor the same large order that would have come your way.

Similarly, a customer or client who likes to order by fax machine will rule you out when they see no fax number on your business card or directory listing. If your business requires the sending or receiving of plans, purchase orders, or documents, then a fax connection is nothing less than imperative.

For similar reasons of convenience, one must have a notary public in or near the office. The master sales manager has to be able to do all of his business in-house, without wasting precious time going outside to finalize routine paperwork. In those lost minutes a customer could get cold feet and back out of a purchase. When the customer is hot to sign a contract, there must be no delays or awkward moments. The thorough master manager, then, knows how crucial it is to have all forms and contracts at his fingertips and plenty of paper in the copying machine.

Staff Dress Code

Unless there are only one or two individuals that need speaking to, the master sales manager may have to impose a dress code for all the people working in his sales office. The object is to have everyone in the sales office looking clean, neat, and reflecting success. There can be no excuses for sloppiness or uncleanliness. Even if the master sales manager has to "inspect his troops" some mornings, the extra time and effort will pay off. Let the salespeople snicker. But when they look smart, they feel smart, and sell smart. Everything that helps make a sales office be more professional can only increase sales.

Royal Restrooms

Always have clean restrooms, especially for the ladies. Nothing can be more repulsive to a customer than to enter a dirty or unkempt restroom in an office. The master sales manager should go to extra lengths to make sure that the restrooms are as clean and well decorated as any other part of the sales office. The ladies' restroom, in particular, should be thoughtfully and tastefully appointed. Any negative impression on a customer will only make the sale that much harder.

The Presentation Room

Your sales office may be set up to facilitate simultaneous customer presentations. You may not have the luxury of separate conference rooms, so there are several points to keep in mind.

THE CLOSING ROOM

In a "closing room" or "sales pit" keep the conference tables far enough apart so that each customer cannot hear distinct conversations that are taking place elsewhere. The buzzing noise from a large area with a lot of closers and customers creates excitement and a positive sales atmosphere, but don't let customers get close enough to hear other sales presentations and negotiations at nearby tables. They will begin comparing another closer's advice, price quotes and financial arrangements. This not only disrupts a closer's presentation, but it can lead to customer resentment and bad feelings between closers.

BEAT THE CLOCK

Do not put clocks on the walls of your presentation or closing room. Just as gambling casinos don't want to advertise what time of day it is, don't make it too easy for a customer to think about being somewhere else. The master sales manager has to keep the customers intrigued with his product and with his sales closer's presentation. The time it takes to close a sale is something you don't want on a customer's mind.

SITTING AT ATTENTION

Unlike the sales office, you don't want the closing room to be "living room comfortable." Plush chairs and soft music here will make the customers overly relaxed at a time when you want them to be attentive to their buying decision. The chairs here can be wooden and straight-backed. Some sales offices use chairs with arms on them so the customer can rest and avoid having to fold his arms—which generates a negative attitude.

NO DISTRACTIONS

Keep all working papers and all sales material, contracts, financial statements, etc., close at hand, but not in plain view of the customers. Any sales materials that are unnecessarily lying around will only have an adverse affect on the customer. Once he's at the closing desk, the customer often has his defenses up and is just waiting for an excuse to build up an objection.

"Mr. Closer, you suggested financing terms on plan A, but according to this company brochure I just found there are better terms for me on plan B."

The carefully built-up momentum of the closer has been disrupted by materials that he did not want this particular customer to see at that time. A blank contract or work sheet lying on a table could similarly intimidate a customer in the same way a hypodermic needle sitting on a doctor's desk can unnerve a patient. To ensure that the closer only produces what he wants, when he wants it, have an uncluttered closing desk where all materials are out of sight and reach of customers.

THE CLOSING TABLE

There are several schools of thought concerning closing tables. Many professional closers prefer the intimacy of round ones, while others prefer the authoritative presence established by rectangular or square ones.

With a round table a closer can lean toward the more eager spouse or business partner and establish a two-against-one majority to press for the sale. When the closer is likely to confront two or more resistant buyers, however, a square table, with chairs spaced far apart, is preferable. This way the closer won't feel "surrounded" by the difficult customer, and won't be as pressured to consider the customer's demands. Instead, the closer will be in a better position to hold firm and negotiate with less intimidation. No matter what its shape, the table had better be solid. The deal will feel like a backroom swindle if it's consummated on a rickety card table. (Make the closing table as solid as a banker's desk.)

RUNNING A PROFESSIONAL SALES OFFICE

Don't Use Time Clocks

There is no reason to use time clocks. If a master manager can't get his office staff to arrive on time for work, then he's not worth his salt. Time clocks might have their place in a large factory, but not in a professional sales office. Every person who works in the sales office should possess the enthusiastic winning spirit of their master sales manager. There is simply no time for tardiness.

It is true that when the cat's away the mice will play. But the master manager is a tiger, not a cat. His highly motivated closers work like men, not mice. A time clock only lends a rat race flavor to what should feel more like a sports clubhouse or a military war room. The closer who keeps punching a time clock will only end up killing time.

The Sales Manager and His Employer

The master sales manager, no matter how dominant a personality he might have, must acknowledge the superior position of his "boss." The boss (the owner or president of the company), on his part, must acknowledge that the sales manager is the expert in knowing and motivating his sales closers. A true master manager won't step on the top brass' toes, and they, in turn, will respect his turf. There will be times, however, when the field marshal and chief of staff don't see eye to eye. When this happens, both parties should withdraw to their lines and see if one of them happens to be overstepping their bounds just a bit. If a manager is producing good results, the owner should not keep him on a short leash. If the manager constantly wants to overturn corporate policies, then it is time for him to start his own corporation.

How to Treat Office Personnel

The master sales manager should treat the secretaries and other support staff members with the same respect reserved for the closers. The premise behind this is that no one feels second class in his sales office, so no one does second-rate work. The star closer and the typist are both important members of a winning team.

The Office Manager Defined

The office manager is not the sales manager. He or she is in the sales office to keep all the paper work and regular office procedures running smoothly. In a busy office, the sales manager would be lost without a competent office manager. The office manager should keep track of all records and sales contracts so that the master sales manager is free to proceed with his job of getting sales.

The office manager works for the master sales manager, not the other way around. When an office manager thinks that he or she can run a professional sales force better than the master sales manager, then the whole sales company suffers from the twisted chain of command.

The Master Sales Manager's Off Hours

What are the duties of a master sales manager after he leaves the office? First, the manager is always on duty because of his personal obligations to his sales team. The sales manager is the one that all the closers turn to whenever they need a personal banker, a marriage counselor, or cleric.

Secondly, the manager's hours away from the sales office are still not his alone. He is always representing his sales company, and forever looking for new ideas to boost sales. The master sales manager is married to his profession, and his wife may not appreciate this "other woman." The manager's children may want dad to loosen up a bit at family outings, but he is a walking public relations asset for his firm even at the ballpark or picnic grounds. He is a salesman, a master closer, and a leader, seven days a week. He never turns off his powers of persuasion and charm. You can take a master manager out of the sales office, but you can't take the sales office out of the master manager.

When to Give Bonuses

QUESTION: *When should a master sales manager give out bonuses and other "rewards" to his office personnel?*
ANSWER: *At every opportunity!*

The reward system is an important shot in the arm to any sales office. It shows the office staff that the master sales manager not only notices jobs well done, but also appreciates them.

QUESTION: *Won't bonuses to select individuals cause jealousy and resentment?*
ANSWER: *This is America.*

Let a mediocre closer, who hasn't earned a bonus in years, go to the Soviet Union, where he'll fit right in. Given in the right spirit, the bonus to an individual will only spur others on to greater efforts. No one will accuse closers Smith and Jones of being the manager's pets when reports of their territories' success are presented at a sales meeting for all to see—and to emulate.

It is a good policy to release some positive statistics every once in a while, and then throw around some bonuses to everyone in the sales office. Those unexpected envelopes make it feel like Christmas in July. Suddenly, everyone in the office is gushing with enthusiasm and pride. This excitement is passed along to the customers, which, in turn, produces the surge in sales that the master manager was orchestrating all along.

What goes around, comes around. That investment in bonuses to the staff could come back to the firm twofold in doubled sales revenues. Those master managers who don't hand out much verbal praise know that these bonuses speak a lot louder than words.

Dealing with Gossip

The master sales manager must deal with "petty" sales office gossip that could quickly grow into a destructive wedge driven between members of the sales team. The first thing that the master sales manager must do is find out the source of the rumor, privately confront the person or persons involved, and separate fact from fiction. Then the manager should immediately address the problem, and "nip it in the bud," quelling the rumor before it gets out of hand and disrupts the flow of office performance.

The Lord knows that closers are as human as anyone else— perhaps more so—and that many of the ugliest rumors about Joe's affair with Carl's wife, or Fred's kickback scheme with a corporate client, are absolutely true. The master manager knows when to discretely call for outside help, like counselors or lawyers, and when to try to smooth things over himself. Even if a rumor proves untrue, the manager must know when it is time to arrange for the "transfer" of a particular closer, or employee who caused too many distractions.

The master sales manager has to have his ear to the ground all the time, but this can be difficult for the more aloof types of managers, who are not as close to their closers as others. In this case the master manager will often develop an agent for intelligence gathering. This agent is often an assistant manager, or a trusted, veteran closer, who serves as the ears of the master manager to pick up and pounce on trouble before it gets out of hand.

Timing can be especially crucial when a manager is faced with the problem of having two of his office personnel battling an "in-house quarrel." The master manager will get the feuding individuals into his office, sit them down in chairs facing each other, and let the combatants settle their differences. This "settling" might take ten minutes or two hours, but it will all be worthwhile. If the problem is resolved and both parties can shake hands, then there will be peace once more in the office. Otherwise, the manager may have to decide on who was guilty, and give one or both parties their walking papers. The manager has to step in as referee early enough to prevent the entire staff from taking sides and ruining the cooperative spirit of the sales team that is so crucial to success.

Planning Sales Projections

The master sales manager plans his sales projections and sets up his game plan along the lines of company goals worked out with senior management. The master sales manager's job is to reach, or even surpass, the stated sales projection. Alone, or perhaps with the help of a trusty "Sidekick," the master manager sits down to plan his attack:

1. He will divide the upcoming sales year ahead into months.
2. He will analyze the monthly potential of each of his sales closers.
3. He will review his product inventory to see what is available for each month, setting up monthly sales quotas based accordingly.

4. He will draw up charts to reflect each month's sales goals, and indicate at regular meetings whether or not those goals are being reached.
5. He will take action to be sure the goals are more likely to be met the following month.

As organized as he is, the master manager should never be the victim of too much planning or unrealistic expectation. He will take into consideration each individual closer, the territories, and monthly trends, so that all stated goals are challenging, yet perfectly feasible.

Keeping the Sales Office in Shape

All of the previous discussion about decorating the inside and outside of the sales office would be in vain if it will not be maintained in "tiptop" shape. Sure, there is a custodian on the premises, but the final responsibility lies with the sales manager. A master sales manager has to have a handle on everything that goes on around the sales office, whether flickering light fixtures are not being replaced, or whether floors are dangerously slippery on Monday mornings.

Along with bonuses for sales, there should be an "Environmental Prize" for the employee showing the most concern for the sales office and grounds. Encourage the entire staff to eliminate soft drink cans, empty cups or dirty ashtrays from desktops. Closers should spot and report any cracks in the ceiling, tear in the wallpaper or stain on the carpet before a customer does.

Never forget that selling is an emotional and psychological exercise; not merely a mechanical, mathematical one. A clean, well-kept environment picks up everyone's spirits and fosters pride in one's nine-to-five "home." The customer is a "guest" in that "home," and any doubts about the "hospitality" or professionalism in the office will make a customer uncomfortable, and will invariably lead to lost sales.

How to Start and End a Selling Season

The master sales manager will start and end his selling season with an extra dose of enthusiasm. The sales manager has to get everyone in his sales office excited about a new selling season, and keep them motivated right down to the last minute of his selling calendar. Everyone works best in rhythm, and a master manager keeps his whole staff moving in rhythm to the necessary pace of the campaign.

Another sure-fire way to inspire the sales team is to keep good office staff around year after year. By showing them respect and letting them immediately know any important company policy decision, your staff will feel involved. The well-set patterns of a master manager become comforting and easy to fall into, no matter how challenging sales quotas might be. And nothing makes a sales office more solid and successful than steady, loyal, and dedicated personnel. To keep these productive employees coming back, the master sales manager has to keep them enthusiastic about sales, the entire team operation, and, even more importantly, about themselves.

The master sales manager lets his good people know that they are growing, not stagnating. Their salaries and bonuses should say that, but another cost efficient way is via the staff's responsibilities. As the master manager annually deepens his personal relationships with his loyal sales team, so should the sense that the veteran closers have more say and more weight in decision making.

The office clerical staff has to be enthusiastic about their duties as well. Fired-up clerical people keep the sales closers' morale up, while an endless procession of interchangeable office staff can dampen the loyalties of the best closers.

The enthusiasm at the start of the selling season has to be charged with promise and potential, challenge and confidence. At season's end there ought to be a note of satisfaction and accomplishment, even if goals were not one hundred percent.

Any adversity has to be turned into an advantage, into a challenging obstacle that the sales team can get pumped up about overcoming. Just as the sports fan will say, "Wait 'til next year," the master manager must fire up his staff to be ready and willing to achieve even better sales figures and to "go get 'em" in the new sales season.

WHAT TO LOOK FOR WHEN HIRING SALES CLOSERS

When building up one's staff of closers there is nothing more important than gathering the finest professionals available. Any ordinary, everyday manager can look through resumes and hire based on past records and other superficial criteria. However, it is the master manager that uses instinct and savvy to get the people that will work best for HIS distinct style of sales team.

There are ten points to follow when hiring closers:

1. Listen to the Sales Closer's Story

When the sales manager sits down in his office to interview a potential sales closer, the very first thing that he has to learn is to be a good listener. There are two main reasons for this. First of all, the sales closer is nervous, and in his nervousness he is liable to make uncharacteristic mistakes in telling you why he wants the job and why he's qualified for it.

The master sales manager should not present a list of predictable questions so the practiced closer can "perform" well on cue. The master manager will just sit there, keep silent and listen. The closer will be forced to elaborate, to stray from his prepared "sales pitch." The closer will see that he's not bowling over an easy mark with his planned presentation. With only the prompt, "Go on," the closer is forced to either begin lying or begin telling the truth. Either way, in these circumstances, some hidden facts about the closer's background and personality will eventually come out.

The second reason for the manager's passive listening stance is to see if the prospective employee is an effective closer. By attentively listening and observing, the master sales manager can learn a lot about the sales closer sitting in front of him. Of course, the closer would like to engage the manager in pleasant conversation, and sell him on congeniality rather than product benefit. The manager who doesn't fall for this trap can sit back and rate the closer for his professional abilities as well as for his charm.

2. Read the Sales Closer's Body Language

When the master sales manager is interviewing a sales closer, he notices everything about him or her, from the brand of watch right down to the shine on the shoes. The observant manager will notice if the closer is well groomed; if he has had a manicure, haircut, shave; or if he is suffering from a hangover, or a hard life. A manager should be able to detect this within minutes of their first meeting.

When listening to the pace and pitch of the closer's voice, the master sales manager does not forget to also read the language of the prospect's eyes, hands, and body movements. If the sales closer's eyes dart around the room, or if the sales closer won't look the manager directly in the eyes, then there is obviously some problem. It could be that the closer is lying about something, or he or she is just plain embarrassed to be in the position of asking for a job. The master manager will find out the truth, rather than making a quick judgement and missing out on hiring a potential all-star closer.

The master sales manager also watches the closer's hands. Are the fingers steady and relaxed, or are they nervously grasping things? Shaking or sweating hands could mean a health problem, nervousness, or that the potential sales closer is lying. Body movements tell similar things, so look for twitching, restlessness, or the continual crossing of legs. The sales manager has to observe everything, and not hire a solid resume or an attractive face. The manager's job depends on the sales closer, and that closer had better be good enough to depend on.

What if a sales closer is so smooth and such a good actor that he or she is hiding all of the telltale signs of trouble? Don't worry, everyone makes hiring mistakes. Besides, if that "actor" did such a great job covering up inexperience or some health problem, then don't be surprised if he or she doesn't "act" their way into the top closer's position.

3. Run a Background Check

Always run a background check on your potential sales closers. Even if a master sales manager has the gut feeling to hire a sales closer on the spot, usher him into the waiting room and make some important calls to various authorities and former employers. The background check will protect the manager and his sales company from future problems. The extra time and effort that goes into this background check is more than worth it, in many ways. For instance, the sales closer being interviewed might have a warrant out for his arrest in another state, or he might have just gotten fired from another sales job for financial or personal misconduct, or he could be a professional con man jumping from job to job.

These kinds of problems can be eliminated before they begin if known about in advance of the actual hiring. The master sales manager's job is to have a successful, powerful, and enthusiastic professional sales team, and it's impossible to reach this goal, if even one of the sales closers proves to be a troublemaker. A master sales manager knows that he's not a doctor, psychiatrist, or minister who can reform or save that "bad apple" and mold him into a productive closer. The master manager has enough molding to do with the healthy new recruits with clean backgrounds. He can't afford to extend himself, and spend the company's time on the problematic prospect of running a social welfare agency along with a sales force.

A master sales manager might not fire an employee when discovering the same flaw that would have prevented the closer's hiring in the first place. Once the manager/closer relationship is established, the manager has a professional obligation to help out the troubled closer. If a sales manager lets a genuine sales talent with a troubled background walk out the door without offering any help or encouragement, then the manager involved is not just prudent—but paranoid.

4. Look for That Special Spirit

Listen to the tone of voice, and watch the eyes when interviewing, to pick up that special master sales closer's spirit. When a master sales closer is interviewing for a sales position, his talents will show. The master sales manager should make mental notes during the interview, remembering the stronger qualities and writing them down on paper after the interview is over. The manager must try to tell exactly where this or that sales closer could or couldn't fit into his total sales force.

If the interviewed closer is "burned out," having lost all of his or her competitive spirit, it will definitely show in facial expressions, the eyes and the voice. A master sales manager has to judge if such a sales closer has any glowing coals left that might be stirred back into a full-fledged fire. A veteran closer often has the skills and experience to be worth such efforts on the part of a manager. If the master manager feels that the closer's coals are ashen and cold, then he will not take on even the most experienced salesperson. Such a spiritually frigid closer can throw cold water on the flames of the rest of the force.

5. See Whether the Closer Has Determination

Step one in checking for the prospective closer's drive and determination is noting how much the prospect wants the job. There are three simple ways that a master sales manager can find out:

First, tell the interviewee that he's probably not strong enough to be on the sales force that is being assembled. Tell him that the sales force will be made up of only power hitters, and that he just doesn't have the track record to qualify. After making this statement, the manager should sit back and let the sales closer try to sell himself. The master sales manager will then see for himself if the prospect is a quitter, or a fighter that wants the job, and deserves it too.

Second, an unconvinced sales manager can try the prospect's patience and perseverance with programmed delays. He will first tell the sales closer to come back to the sales office the next day to complete the interview and evaluation process. If, and when, the sales closer shows up, the manager should put his appointment off still another day, making it two delays in a row. If the sales closer shows up on the third day, and arrives with the same excitement and determination, then a master sales manager will hire him.

Third, the sales manager should tell the prospective closer that he will only be used on a trial basis, until he proves himself. (A probation period, if you will, as found in other professions.) The sales manager should express doubt that the prospect will pass the trial period and make it to the sales team. The manager should even act like the offer of a probationary position was a generous gesture on his part. If the sales closer still wants to sell on these terms, and expresses gratitude for the opportunity, and confidence that the trial period will prove his or her worth; if everything else about the candidate checks out, then a manager ought to hire this prospect on the spot.

The fact is that sales managers need closers with a high level of determination and tenacity, and the only way to measure this quality is with the sometimes painful litmus test of the interview and of challenges like those described above.

6. See Whether the Closer Can Take Criticism

If the sales closer cannot take constructive criticism, then he or she is more temperamental than most in a field where egos are all too important. Almost every good closer thinks of himself as God's gift to the sales profession. Every good closer can learn humility if the lesson comes from a master sales manager.

The fastest way for a master sales manager to see if a sales closer is overly sensitive about constructive criticism is right up front at the initial hiring interview. For example, the master sales manager might start off by telling a prospective sales closer who is wearing a lot of good jewelry that he doesn't want his sales closer to "glitter" too much. Or, the sales manager might inform the prospect that cowboy boots are not allowed to be worn during work hours by anyone on his sales team. If the sales closer takes issue with these criticisms, or expresses even mild resentment at being told what to wear, then the master sales manager knows not to hire him. If the prospect is negative or combative in a small issue, like dress, then he or she will surely be as resistant, or even worse, in bigger issues of corporate policy down the road.

The master sales manager has to maintain control, and he has to establish it from the very start—even if he's rather partial to cowboy boots.

7. See Whether the Closer Believes in Himself

No matter how much motivational skill the sales manager can muster, one must start out with a subject who has some measure of confidence in his or her abilities. The sales manager can't always find out in one interview if the prospective closer believes in himself. But one can get a pretty good idea about the closer by asking the following questions:

1. Ask the sales closer what his goals are in life; what it is that he's working toward. Almost any answer will suffice if it is spoken without hesitation and with conviction.

2. Enquire of the prospective sales closer why he wants to quit his other sales job and come to work for the company he is interviewing with now. See if his is floundering restlessly or driving his career forward.

3. Ask the sales closer directly just why he believes in himself. As vague and disturbing as the question is, it will be quite instructive to see if the closer responds with confident humor, or with serious panic. If the closer believes in himself, he will undoubtedly be confident in his statements.

The average sales closer is not used to this kind of personal questioning and caring from a seasoned sales manager, and will more than likely let down his guard. When that happens, five minutes of heart-to-heart talk is worth more than an hour of guarded responses.

These questions are extremely important so that the sales manager can gauge the confidence level of the prospective closer, to know if he has the potential to be made into a successful salesman. If that self-belief has been tarnished and lost by the sales closer over a period of time, the sales manager has to make a decision whether to attempt a polishing job or not.

8. See Whether the Closer Has an Alcohol or Drug Problem

With today's statistics, a sales manager owes it to his company, and to the other closers, to find out if a prospective sales closer has an alcohol or drug problem. An outright lush or junkie won't be showing up for the interview, so the manager has to be slick enough to pick out the careful, but habitual, substance abuser who many seem high powered and confident on the outside. That person is an accident waiting to happen, come weekends and holidays. In today's fast and furious sales world, the abuser is very likely to be among the top prospects.

The sales closer with a problem will not be telling the truth on this one, and it's totally up to the sales manager's instincts to discover the symptoms and to bring up the subject. When the manager asks the closer if he has a bit of a drinking or drug problem, he had better say it in a genuinely caring manner. With the help of God, and the services of a good counselor, a talented, but troubled, closer can produce miraculous sales for a master sales manager that courageously believes in him.

9. See Whether the Closer Is Honest

How can a sales manager find out if a sales closer is honest? It is nearly impossible. The sales manager can run a background check on the closer to see if he wasn't dishonest (and caught) in the past. Even if the closer was a swindler earlier in life, people can change. Dishonest sales closers have become good, honest citizens, and honest sales closers have become crooks, virtually overnight. The sales manager cannot protect himself one hundred percent on this question, and he is sure to get burned every once in a while.

The master sales manager has to remember to stick to proper rules and values, always leading his staff as the prime example of fairness and honesty. A sales manager is not a master sales manager if he operates any differently. By being true to his word and his principles, the master sales manager will insure that his honest sales closers will far outnumber any dishonest ones.

10. Look for Loyalty and Dedication

If a job candidate has moved around from one sales force to another, especially if he or she has left jobs with histories of employee turnover, one can assume that the prospect has little capacity for team loyalty. If an untried sales prospect has switched schools and addresses, it might also portend a vagabond who will not be worth your investing much time and effort.

The only way sales manager foster true loyalty and dedication from sales closer is by first showing it to them. The closer must know that the manager will stand by him when he gets into a bit of trouble. After having been led by example, sales closer will generally go out of their way to stay loyal to their manager, and to the firm. Most sales closers want to be part of a truly professional team, a winning team that they can look back on in the years to come and say, "I was a member of that famous sales force."

Sales closers know that to have a top caliber sales force, loyalty and teamwork are the key factors to make it all work. Nothing succeeds like success, and often that first positive quarterly report of sales begins to push the closers together as a winning team. Inevitably, that new cohesion focuses on their leader, and the force comes to acknowledge the orchestrator of their successful team effort—the master sales manager.

KEEPING TABS ON THE SALES CLOSERS

Setting Down the Rules

Have every sales closer sign a standardized statement that lists all of the rules governing the sales office and the sales operation. These Rules of Conduct should be typed up, and written in simple, jargon-free English. The statement should basically list a number of do's and don'ts to be followed by everyone on the staff. These Rules of Conduct should contain basic, cardinal rules, making clear what forms of business and personal conduct are not tolerated around the sales office.

The Rules of Conduct should include:

1. There is to be no extracurricular socializing with sales closers or sales office staff of the opposite sex.
2. Lateness to sales meetings will not be tolerated; excuses—and they better be good ones—must be called in prior to meeting time.
3. No possession or use of alcoholic beverages or illegal drugs will be tolerated on the office premises; manifest abuse of such substances are grounds for immediate dismissal.
4. Every customer must be treated with the greatest respect; you will defer to the manager when encountering problems, rather than returning any customer's misbehavior.

This list of do's and don'ts is invaluable. When a sales closer breaks one of these rules, all the sales manager has to do is pull out this signed Rules of Conduct statement from the closer's file. It is then up to the manager to decide what to do next. At least the closer, who signed the statement, now knows that he doesn't have a leg to stand on in his defense, and that his job security is all in the hands of the sales manager. Firings, or even severe reprimands, aren't always easy to administer. Flashing such an agreement before a guilty closer, however, squarely places the manager in the right.

Stick By the Rules

The master sales manager has to stick by his own operating rules for the sales office, and he cannot be "wishy washy" in executing penalties for breaking those rules.

If found guilty of misbehavior himself, a master sales manager will call a meeting, openly confess and resign. He or she can then proceed to walk out with his or her head held high. The chances are good that the staff and ownership will ask the manager to reconsider—if the infraction is not too severe. A master manager can turn a potential disaster, such as showing up drunk at the office, into a show of integrity by thus showing that he was ready to pay the ultimate price for breaking his own rule.

A master sales manager has to be as fair—but as firm—as a good army general. He cannot make exceptions, or bend the sales office rules to fit the situation. The sales manager is not running a popularity contest, he is running a professional sales force that has a life and spirit of its own. His job is to keep the sales force operating together as a winning team. Any preferences, in terms of undeserved bonuses or special favors, that are shown to any one of the team members, will only destroy the sales force in the long run.

The sales manager who sets down in writing the Rules of Conduct for the sales office had better follow them to the letter himself. If there are changes to be made in any rules, as circumstances dictate, then the manager has to enact these changes openly and aboveboard.

Lock Up Important Papers

As much as a manager trusts his staff, he must be protected against unscrupulous, ambitious people who work for rival firms, or who want to open up a competing operation. Always lock up important papers and customer mailing lists when away from the sales office. These priceless lists and customer contracts are much too valuable and tempting to be left lying around. The sales manager's desk and files should be locked and such documents should be secured in the company's computer.

This type of information is what a professional sales organization runs on, and the risk of losing this information to any competitor is worth the time it takes to lock it up and secure it. A master sales manager is aware that in business there will always be people out there who don't play by the rules. One can be trusting enough to lend one's second car out to a closer with car trouble, but not so naive as to keep valuable documents in easy access.

CONTROLLING THE CLOSERS

Have Regular Sales Meetings

The primary way that a master sales manager controls the energy and pace of his master sales closers is by having regular sales meetings at a set hour. It cannot be stated strongly enough how important regular sales meetings are to the working rhythm of any professional sales force. Sales meetings are to sales teams what half-times are to basketball teams, huddles are to football teams, and regrouping is to a field general.

Sales meetings educate and motivate sales closers in three important ways:

1. They bring the whole sales force together, even if scattered around the state or region, allowing them to regroup as a unified team.
2. They allow the closers and manager to rethink strategies, and make adjustments in tactics according to new marketing developments in the field.
3. They bring closers back to their inspirational master manager, and allow them to re-chart newly crystallized goals that rejuvenate them and keep them from closer burn out. As if he's had a tune-up, the closer should pull out of the sales meetings all souped-up and energized about selling his product. Sales meetings keep a closer running at his peak.

The master sales manager establishes control over his sales closers by first insisting that everyone be on time to these meetings, whether they are every morning at seven o'clock for a local establishment, or once a month at 4 p.m. for a national distribution chain. There cannot be any absentees or tardiness. A master sales manager knows that if a closer's body is not present and accounted for, his or her heart isn't likely to be either.

Furthermore, a master sales manager establishes his control at these sales meetings by demanding, and getting, everyone's attention. The different style managers discussed above will conduct their meetings like classrooms, rallies, or war councils—but in none of these meetings will closers be catching up on their sleep. Beyond roll call, a master manager knows how to engage closers individually, calling on his charges to respond to specific questions. A full range of effects, from visual aids to jokes to veiled threats, are manipulated by the master manager to keep the sales staff at the edge of their seats.

The sales meeting is also used to its best advantage when it doubles as a public forum. Even if inventory information is printed and distributed to the staff, use the dramatic occasion of the meeting to spell out significant trends, ominous warnings or optimistic predictions. This is the chance to publicly give out closer-of the-month awards, bonuses, and other incentives. After a sales chart has flashed on the screen, follow up with a slide of Closer Cal's new baby girl or slides of last month's company barbecue. Mixing business with pleasure makes business more pleasurable. Mixing family news with company notes makes the company more like family.

Help Closers with Financial Problems

If a deserving sales closer needs financial help, or has problems with his personal bills, a master sales manager will get involved. It is taxing emotionally and financially to commit oneself this way to an employee, but remember that this is another significant way for a sales manager to win the undying loyalty of a sales closer. Helping a closer out with personal finances doesn't have to mean floating him a five thousand dollar loan or paying her overdue dental bills. It does mean getting involved, often helping the closer become financially organized and fiscally responsible. Dealing with everyday business transactions does not give the closers a facility with personal financial details, so many of them greatly appreciate a master sales manager who can sit down with them and work out a financial game plan. Once the manager has stepped in to be the closer's personal banker or accountant, the manager should follow through with periodic checks.

By going this extra mile for a sales closer, the master sales manager accomplishes two important goals. First, he gets his sales closer back into a good selling frame of mind, freeing him from the kind of pressures or uncertainties that would hamper his career and productivity. Secondly, the master sales manager has now involved himself right in the closer's personal life. He has practically become a big brother, or a father figure, whose judgement and directives are sure to be respected and followed. There is a tremendous amount of positive impact when a closer begins telling his peers what a great guy the manager is, how much the manager really cares and how much he knows about managing money.

Write Sales Reports to Spouses

Make bi-monthly calls and mail regular reports addressed to the closer and their spouse to get the whole family involved. Some closers will think this is a somewhat sneaky thing to do, but it accomplishes important goals. First, the earning information prevents the closer's paycheck from being wiped out on secret, and possibly destructive, vices. Second, the spouse can now lend moral support to rally his, or her, partner through a low period, or cheer the husband or wife on when the commissions and bonuses are rolling in.

A master manager knows that behind every successful closer there is a good woman or man backing them up on the home front. This tactic doesn't apply to single closers, even if they live at home. (They'd resent such notes home; it would seem like getting report cards again.) For many closers, the reportage shouldn't go on during the entire selling season, lest it lose its effectiveness.

Have Regular Sales Parties

The sales manager should have regular sales parties to relieve tensions and to keep up team spirit. Well-done parties keep the excitement alive in the sales force throughout the selling season, keeping the pitch high enough to out-produce the competition.

The master sales manager also uses parties to get to know his sales closers and their families. He can observe the sales closers' actions and see which ones drink too much, get too loud and rambunctious, or lose control and make fools of themselves. It is often in such an informal environment that a sales closer will first approach the manager to discuss problems that would never come up in the official setting of the sales office.

People can let their hair down at an office party or outing, but a master sales manager will never let himself get carried away. He has to always maintain control and set a good example for others. Remember, everyone always has an eye on the leader; rivals are just waiting and watching for a mistake.

Have an Ear to the Ground

The master sales manager should always have his ear to the ground, always knowing what is going on inside and outside the sales office. If a master sales manager doesn't know what is going on around him, such as petty jealousies and infighting, power plays, "occasional" cocaine use, office affairs, financial cheating etc., he is at a marked disadvantage. He will not be able to contain disasters, never mind nip them in the bud.

A major way that the master sales manager maintains control is by his uncanny ability to know all the dirty secrets and to act decisively to protect the firm from harm. Even a master sales manager has got to have help to keep on top of everything that goes on around his sales force. For the manager to know all, he obviously has to have inside people who keep him up to date. If the idea of having intelligence agents or informants among the staff is distasteful, perhaps you are not aware of how brutal the sales world can be and how vulnerable a "powerful" position like sales manager can be. "All is fair in love and war," and the sales world is a combination of love and war.

One cannot hire closers just to be spies, and even the friendliest of assistant managers won't be as effective a watchdog as a fellow closer. How, then, does the master manager engage these all-important secret agents? For one thing, those closers whom the manager has helped personally can be counted on to return favors with significant tidbits of information. It simply has to be made clear to them that their discreet help in information gathering is greatly needed and appreciated. If they find themselves breaking the trust of individual closers on occasion, they are to realize that their services help all the closers in the long run.

Furthermore, it can be guaranteed that in any sales office there will always be people who volunteer information to the sales manager. A master manager knows that such information is offered to curry favor or destroy rivals, so that it is to be taken with a grain of salt. The master manager should keep both these lines of information open and protected, so that he can always depend on several extra sets of ears and eyes.

Know the Closer's Income Tax Situation

You can lead a closer to his tax forms, but you can't make him pay. The master sales manager should know about the federal tax situation of each of his sales closers for two reasons: *(1) to insure that the sales firm is not implicated in any misbehavior, and (2) to know that closers are not headed for debtor's prison in their soon-to-be-repossessed BMW.*

Not every closer will be approaching the manager for financial help, yet the master sales manager wants to extend his financial control over his sales closers by knowing how each one stands on his or her federal income tax obligations. If a sales closer hasn't paid income taxes in a number of years, or is slowly getting over his head in debt, then a responsible sales manager should find out. There are several ways to find out this information. Here are two:

1. Come tax time, all the closers can be offered the services of a single accounting firm offering attractive group rates. Those rates are kept attractively low by the manager who, in turn, is informed about any closers with financial troubles.
2. A second way to get involved in the sales closers' finances is to offer a tax fund that works like a bank's Christmas Club. A small amount can be withheld from paychecks and, earning interest in a special fund, used later to help the closer pay his taxes.

Of course, the closer may be reluctant to reveal his current and previous tax returns. Even if the closer chooses not to cooperate with the manager's fact-finding schemes, the sales manager, at least, knows where the closer stands and to be wary of potential problems. The closer, for his part, knows that his sales manager is no dummy, and that he is not likely to get away with financial misbehavior.

Show Respect, Receive Respect

With all the talk about keeping tabs on the closer's private and financial life, a master manager never forgets to show his closers genuine trust and respect. Respect gains respect. The master sales manager takes the time to listen to a sales closer's problems and suggestions. A closer should feel that he or she has a say in matters, and can apply initiative to help increase sales. A master sales manager will proudly announce at a meeting that a new plan or approach suggested by Closer John or Carole will be put into effect. A closer greatly appreciates the personal space provided by the manager, and a closer who feels important and involved is likely to be a valuable asset to the manager and the entire sales force.

Respect also means that a closer who isn't doing well will be offered extra training, extra attention, and extra caring, rather than a chewing out. When a sales closer makes a mistake, it is his manager's respect that allows the mistake to be forgiven and forgotten. The master sales manager does not merely dole out respect because he's such a great guy. The master manager understands that he can control and regulate a sales closer if he has won his reciprocated respect.

WHAT MANAGERS MUST KNOW ABOUT SALES CLOSERS

1. All sales closers think that they are the very best. The sales manager had better get used to the fact that all closers have large and sensitive egos. Sales closers are professional persuaders; their job is the job of selling people products. When they become master closers at the very top of their profession, they think they can sell anyone and make anybody see things their way. They begin to think that they have all the answers, and that sales managers too must be enamored with their flashes of charm and offers of wisdom.

   A master sales manager can appreciate the confidence behind the inflated ego, knowing that the master closer is successful at what he does.

2. The manager must also know how to tolerate and redirect the master sales closers' very competitive nature. He doesn't try to fight the know-it-all mentality, but properly uses it for the good of the company. When sales production figures are posted, the master sales closers are very concerned about who is listed in the top percentages of the sales force. Even though they may not admit it, serious closers are instinctively competitive. They are not in the selling game just for the salary, the commissions, or the satisfaction of convincing customers that their products are the best, but also for the glory of having

all their fellow closers know how good they really are. A master sales closer will work his tail off faster and harder to outsell his colleague than to receive a sales bonus. Master sales closers want to be recognized when they're on top, and the master sales manager had better do it.

3. Sales managers must also be aware of the closers' propensity to exaggerate. Remember that master sales closers are trained actors, and they like to paint their presentations with the brightest of colors. Now, these embellishments and puffing habits are just that, habits. The master sales manager will condone and even appreciate this communication habit, learning to distinguish between the real and the almost real when dealing with his sales closers. A master sales manager doesn't panic, therefore, when informed about a "terrible misuse of company assets" or a "vicious fight between closers over the weekend." Most likely, someone was only misusing a few dollars worth of the postage meter, and the two closers had only sparred verbally. The master manager will calmly go about confirming the information rather than rushing in to make a mountain out of a molehill.

4. Master sales closers often think that they can do a better job of managing than their own sales manager. All good sales closers feel deep down in their hearts that they could be super sales managers, if only given the chance. This intuitive feeling might prove to be true in some cases, but a master sales manager—with a sizable ego of his own—is not likely to appreciate self-appointed assistant managers.

The master sales manager will realize that even the louder, more vociferous closers are not threatening his position of authority. They are merely acting out their managerial fantasies. If his top closers didn't feel like dominating a meeting every once in a while, a master manager would think that there is something seriously wrong with his sales force. It's good to have closers who don't always agree with their sales manager. The true master manager will take the time to listen to his closers' criticism, hoping to learn something that will help sales production.

> NOTE: *Sometimes a manager will go along with a questionable suggestion from the closers just to show his flexibility. Instead of an "I told you so" speech after the suggestion fails, the master manager will tactfully remind the closers that he did not think much of the proposal from the start. The manager should go on to say that he implemented the proposal nonetheless because he does think the world of his staff. Thus softly humbled, the sales staff is now ever more ready to be led by the wisdom and experience of their master sales manager.*

The sales manager who has stocked his sales force with "yes men" who always agree with him, or who has cowed all his closers into submission with a dictatorial style, undoubtedly has a sales force that is not producing its best. The master manager knows how to step back just enough for innovation and creativity, without withdrawing and leaving a vacuum for undirected ideas and anarchy.

5. Most sales closers are as lazy as a manager allows. Sure, the average closer will sell to their regular, assigned customers, but getting a salesperson out in the field to hustle up new accounts can be difficult, if not impossible. The master sales manager understands this natural fear and loathing for cold selling on the part of his closers, so he has to push, pry, pull, threaten and bribe his staff every single day to get them into that extra territory where success resides.

6. Managers must know that few closers are happy with their assigned accounts or territory. Several sales closers will always insist that they were given the short end of the stick while the manager's favorites were fed the "lay-downs" (pushover customers and automatic accounts). The sales manager must understand that it is only human nature to see the grass as

greener in the other fellow's yard. As soon as assignments are parcelled out, a master sales manager must point out that the territories and account loads of each closer are as equally divided as possible. The manager should back up such assertions with graphic aids and stop the corrosive grumbling, once and for all, at the beginning of the selling season.

NOTE: On occasion there is some truth behind the bickering of a closer. Some sales managers will play favorites, sending a rookie closer, or a closer he doesn't personally care for, out into virgin, even barren sales territory. There is no excuse whatsoever for this kind of managerial tactic, as it will alienate other members of the sales staff. The manager shouldn't assign a closer to unpromising accounts as a means of courting his resignation. Let him come right out and fire the guy if he really doesn't like him, or has legitimate reasons to do so.

In general, a master manager understands that his closers are only human. They might have self-destructive habits, they might think no boss is fair, they might misinterpret a "go-fer" job to get something at the post office as a demeaning "punishment" on the part of the manager. At times a master manager feels that he's dealing with a group of children instead of adults. Well, a manager must have the patience and understanding of a parent. The master manager will also develop the love of a parent, seeing his sales people through all kinds of emotional rough spots while "raising" them to be highly productive master sales closers. He doesn't try to fight the know-it-all mentality, but properly channels it for the good of the company.

CHAPTER 3

Preparing the Sales Team:
Giving Sales Meetings
to Motivate and Educate

The primary objective for those all-important sales meetings is to establish the sales manager's control over his sales closers. Without power and control flowing from that podium, the sales manager will never achieve the mastery needed for business success. No matter how effective he is on the one-to-one, the master manager is able to project leadership to the collective group, to make the sales meeting the effective stage for his strong, focused will. No pile of memos by a competent bureaucrat can create the aura of control that a master manager projects at the sales meeting.

THE SEVEN MAIN REASONS FOR THE
ALL-IMPORTANT SALES MEETING

1. Control

The deputy of control is discipline. Demand that these sales meetings be at a certain place, at a specified time, and with the full office dress code in effect. Before conducting the meeting himself, the master sales manager should involve others by assigning various duties to closers. These might include:

    a. Taking attendance
    b. Reading the minutes of the last meeting

   c. *Recording the minutes of the current*
     meeting
   d. *Handing out relevant copies or*
     computer printouts
   e. *Seeing that there are adequate chairs*
     in the meeting room, that the micro-
     phone is in order and that a fresh glass
     of water is at the podium

NOTE: Early mornings are the best time for sales meetings, because that is when everyone is alert. One cannot exercise control over closers when their minds and bodies are tired from a day's work.

2. Motivate

Never forget that closers can't sell a thing if they are not excited about themselves and their product. In other words, they have to be constantly motivated, a primary job responsibility of the sales manager. The master sales manager uses his sales meetings as the principle vehicle for motivating his closers. No matter how well the manager does on a one-to-one, sales meetings are the only organized gatherings that occur regularly, where the total sales force can sit down together and focus in a spirited, unified way together toward the same objective.

A sales force that runs in many different emotional directions, without a common cause or purpose, will run out of steam and evaporate in a very few days. Individual bonuses can keep some of the closers motivated some of the time, but only energetic, well-informed sales meetings will keep all of the closers going all of the time. The master sales manager has to use his sales meeting like a political rally or a sports half time show to create excitement and enthusiasm and to focus that team spirit on particular team goals.

3. Educate

Sales meetings should be learning experiences for every sales closer. The master sales manager has to keep the closers up to date on sales and technical developments related to the company's product line. The master sales manager is constantly teaching his closers new sales methods and techniques, and he keeps them engaged all season long, charting their sales, and those of rival divisions and companies. The master sales manager is also a master educator who never allows his educational sessions to become dull or overly technical. By instinct, or by training, such a manager knows how to vary his pitch, make eye contact with all, and keep closers on their toes with questions.

4. Set Specific Goals

Sales meetings are the time and place for the manager to let his sales closers know exactly what is expected of them. Only with an exact figure can a closer feel that he has met, or fallen short of, his company's expectations. The closers should also be privy to the entire division's or company's projections, so that his particular contributions toward those goals can be measured and considered crucial. A realistic game plan must be drawn up for closers and for the entire "team," even though they may involve projections over several months' time. If a sales manager doesn't have a predetermined game plan, with a beginning, middle, and end, then he might as well try to win a regatta in a fast boat without the use of a rudder. Remember, you can't tell someone else where he should be headed unless you know the direction yourself.

Master sales managers let their sales force understand the overall marketing objective, so that everyone involved has a common vision of where they need to be headed to get the job done. With specific goals, a slumping closer can be motivated to catch up, and an over-achieving closer can relax and stave off an early burnout.

5. Reward

If an all-American football player were to make a touchdown in front of all of his teammates and fifty thousand fans, and not one single person cheered or clapped, then that star athlete would walk into the club house, take off his pads, and never play the game again. It doesn't matter if it's a professional ball club, an army of a million men, or a sales team of only four people. When someone performs well, that person wants, and expects, to be acknowledged and rewarded. If prolific sales go unrecognized, even a veteran closer will pick up and go elsewhere.

Sales meetings are the perfect forum for giving out rewards and team recognition. Everyone can get excited by the team success brought on by the star closer's achievements and everyone can feel that they too could produce numbers like that. Even a quieter, more introverted closer will be genuinely honored by the attention, and will be more inclined to give tips to colleagues with whom he might have previously felt competitive. Of course, attention can get addictive. And the master manager knows which egos to feed and how much to feed each one to keep that top achievement level at its peak.

6. *Inform*

The sales meeting is a place to let everyone know what is going on, why it is going on, and how it is going on. Master sales managers, no matter how busy they are, have the ability to explain procedures and give directives effectively and concisely, letting the total sales force in on the news. The closers should come out of a meeting feeling that they know everything relevant about the company, the product, the competition, and developing trends.

Before the sales force hears the competition's new financing or rebate campaign on the radio and begins to wonder what this will force them to do, the master manager informs them of the new development and presents several ways to counterattack. Somehow, a master manager makes information that is familiar to the veterans seem fresh and compelling, as if the listeners were rookies. The manager may keep closers on their toes by suddenly asking Closer John to explain a recent development to the assembled buyers or field representatives who are in from the opposite coast.

7. Regroup

Why does every competitive team sport have a half-time, time outs, or between period breaks? Why, for that matter, do army generals hold war councils in the heat of battle? The answer is that in sports, war, and business, the strategies of the opponents are constantly shifting. A sales manager, too, can feel that the opposition has shifted to a full-court press, a two-minute drill or a kamikaze attack. The sales force cannot operate on past momentum when the opposition has made extreme offensive or defensive moves. The manager must regroup, realign, and readjust the force's movements. A sales meetings allows the manager and closers to analyze the competition's offensive and to coordinate an effective response. A master sales manager, like a good sports coach, will involve his sales closers in his "game plan," making sure that the whole "team" is up on the "play book" for the upcoming quarter.

HOW A MASTER SALES MANAGER ACQUIRES THE "SELF-IGNITING LEADERSHIP ELEMENT"

DEFINITION: The term "self-igniting leadership element" simply means the ability that a person has to motivate and encourage oneself without any external help. This unique ability is found in the makeup and character of ninety-nine percent of all true master sales managers worldwide.

How this leadership element is acquired by an individual is a complex matter. First of all, every human being, whether born rich or poor, whether black, white, Hispanic, Asian, or other, possesses at least one special ability that he or she can use to the benefit of his fellow man. Secondly, this unique talent is more than sufficient to make an individual a very comfortable living.

Sadly, if a young person is raised in an atmosphere where there is no encouragement, no positive reinforcement for that innate gift, the child's lost dreams could well result in a societal nightmare. If, on the other hand, a young person is brought up in a positive, nurturing atmosphere, surrounded by people who encourage that dream, and the curiosity and drive that dreams feed on, then that special talent will eventually surface and the young person can then continue on to develop that gift to the very fullest.

Even if the budding violinist never makes it to a concert hall, or the little slugger never gets past Pony League, that developing human being has, nonetheless, grown up with a positive sense of self. That young adult develops, right along with his or her hormones, a perceptible amount of courage, boldness, sureness, and dedication. These unconditionally loved and non-neurotically nurtured young men and women know that they are special, that with a bit of tenacity they can become the best in the area where they feel their talents are most utilized and appreciated. That sense of being "loved" shines out of these natural leader types, and the masses of less fortunate people feel enriched by just being in the orbit of these charismatic "stars."

Most of us who don't develop our innate gifts, who don't enjoy the fruits of our inborn talents, are those who have not discovered our gifts. Despite this handicap, we can at least observe others who are successful and latch on to a dream with self-developed ambition. If one type more than the other (from the profiles featured in chapter one) exudes a cheerful charisma and a positive management style, it is often because the positive manager was swathed in parental approval, encouragement and love from earliest childhood.

If that future closer was nurtured on dreams of the silver screen, or the preacher's pulpit, he might find himself happily fulfilled selling insurance or computer systems. In sales, or any other profession, you are using your natural gifts, and fulfilling your reason for being, when your vocation meets your avocation. You have made it when you come home from work and it just feels right, it fits. The feeling is akin to love, rather than the slow burn of a boring, unchallenging, and bothersome job.

Therefore, when a career and a true talent have found each other, this marriage allows the love to be fruitful and multiply. The person's innate courage and confidence has grown from a small flame to a great fire that can warm and enlighten those who come near. That person has the self-igniting leadership quality of a master manager.

Such is the personal and career background of a master sales manager: one with the talent to lead other people through difficult situations and to get sales closers to demonstrate sales excellence in all types of situations. In other words, master sales managers are individuals who have discovered, nurtured and developed their talent. They may have been born with the potential for charisma, but they also worked on acquiring their special "self-igniting leadership element."

Keep in mind that they were not specifically born into the sales profession, and that being a manager is not for everyone with leadership ability. If that master manager's talents really lay in the engineering or entertainment field, then that person would never have gotten into sales. Money shouldn't be, and never is, the career criterion for a natural leader. The kind of person who becomes a master manager knows instinctively that financial success will follow anything that he or she plunges into.

> NOTE: Earlier in this explanation about the "self-igniting leadership element," it was stated that a young person's environment or setting was crucial, and that a positive atmosphere was the most important factor to be considered. This is why so many immigrants to the United States have thrived in the New World. They had the vision and drive to change their obviously unpleasant life and flee to a place where they could be free and flourish; where their talents were appreciated. I have been fortunate enough to work for such bosses, people from other lands who had to struggle to come here for the opportunity to excel.

Immigrants or Mayflower descendants, we are all confronted with the choice of pursuing comfortable mediocrity, or taking the challenge that might lead to spectacular success or failure. The master sales manager has clearly chosen that second, less chosen path. His choice shows in the character lines in his face, that spark, the "self-igniting leadership element," in his eyes. By simply being around him, you can feel that master managers believe in themselves. And master managers can make the closers who work with them believe in themselves as well.

HOW TO MOTIVATE MASTER SALES CLOSERS

The master sales closer needs motivation, and the average closer always needs to have his self-confidence bolstered. When the manager confirms those very flattering things that the closer is thinking about himself, then something magic happens. A positive power is ignited in the sales closer, a real excitement and enthusiasm. The master sales manager knows just how to stroke those closer egos, and to turn that ignited enthusiasm into greater sales production.

Working on the Closer's Ego

All sales closers have super egos. If they didn't think they could make money on their charm, they would have taken a civil service job or hidden themselves behind a computer. The master sales manager can motivate any sales closer by just pulling him aside, looking him straight in the eye, and saying in the most sincere way, "Closer Bob, out of the whole sales force, you are the only person I can depend on to get a home run, to get a sale today. You, Closer Bob, whether you know it or not, are the leader, the one all the other people look up to. And right now I really need your leadership. Go out there and get me that sale, so I can show the other closers what a true professional can do." Immediately after delivering this adrenaline shot to the ego, the master sales manager should firmly shake the sales closer's hand and walk off without saying another word. This tactic works miracles.

> NOTE: *The tactic above cannot work for every type of closer, nor can it be used on too many closers without being*

*discovered and undermined. Motivating different closers, all
at the same time, is discussed later on in this chapter.*

Using Logic

The master sales manager can use logic to motivate his sales closers
in a number of different ways. For instance, he can privately talk
to a debt-ridden sales closer, and logically explain to him that the
only way to alleviate massive debt is to stop worrying about details
of his budget, and to concentrate only on sales. He should explain
that the answer to all the closer's problems is simply to increase
income by getting more sales. Or, the master sales manager can
motivate a depressed sales closer, in a low selling period, and turn
him around by pulling out the closer's records from past years,
and reminding him of his past triumphs. He transfers all the
closer's emotional problems into the logical realm of statistics,
noting deviations and norms.

"Closer Bill, you were a top producer in periods A, B and C
and you are sure to be one again. Look how you pulled out of
similar slumps last spring and the year before that."

The real issue affecting the closer's performance may be a
problem relationship or marriage, but the master sales manager
knows how to soothe the closer with mathematical and
mechanical "proofs" and advice that guide the sales person back
to a productive path. Using logic, the manager creates an
emotional safe house in the office. Instead of closers bringing their
personal problems to the office, they look forward to coming to
work and checking their emotional baggage at the door.

Using Rewards

The master sales manager knows that if he doesn't reward his sales
closers for doing a good job, his closers will not only start
performing badly, they will eventually move to greener pastures.
No one is going to bust his rear end for the same money he could
get for coasting on cruise control. Just ask the Soviets; they learned
this lesson the hard way. In a sales force, the bastion of Capitalism,

you have to offer capital gains. Cash bonuses, plaques, gifts, and verbal congratulations are all very necessary. It is up to the master manager to decide which "spiffs" and incentives are appropriate for each occasion or landmark in the sales season. Don't forget, if rewards didn't work as motivational tools, then professional ball clubs wouldn't hand out trophies and championship rings, and the armies of the world wouldn't hand out medals and ribbons.

Using Fear

Another great tool that master sales managers use to motivate sales closers is fear. Fear can be used as a cattle prod in either a direct way or an indirect way. An example of the direct way involves the manager telling a sales closer that if he doesn't start selling soon, he won't have a job anymore. Or, fear can be used in a more subtle way. For example, the sales manager can completely ignore a sales closer who is producing poorly. This cold shoulder and icy stare will cause a slow burn in the closer's mind, creating doubts, confusion, anxiety, and the fear of being fired. Fear motivation works, but it has to be executed by a master sales manager who knows what he is doing and to whom he is doing it. If misdirected, this tactic can backfire and make a slumping, but promising, closer panic and quit.

Using Intimidation

Intimidation, different from the fear of firing, can be powerful if used correctly. The master sales manager who uses intimidation to motivate his sales closers had better know how to use it, and he had better be physically and mentally strong enough to back up his actions. One way a master sales manager might intimidate a sales closer is to tell him that he is not yet good enough to work on his sales team, and that the closer needs to learn more salesmanship from the other working closers. Otherwise, the master manager could bring up sensitive subjects, or areas that tend to humble the sales closer.

Perhaps a previous financial bailout on the part of the manager can be used to remind the closer that "he owes," thus he must work harder to pay back old debts and prove deserving of past favors. Remember to use intimidation with care, and not to let it cross over into the realm of humiliation.

Using Pride

Master sales closers are very proud people who love to sell products by mastering the art of persuasion. They don't mind at all if their professional sales reputation precedes them to a new job, and they know that their track record will speak for itself. The master sales manager can use all of the closer's professional pride and arrogance to his advantage, if he is sharp. For instance, the manager could make the proud sales closer a team captain, designating him to show the ropes to the newer sales closers on the force. By giving a proud old pro new responsibility, the master sales manager not only gains control of the closer, but also pushes him into the spotlight where he has to produce to earn his trumpeted reputation.

Using Shame

A master sales manager can shame a sales closer into action with a good old heart-to-heart talk. When certain sales closers need to be motivated, sales manager tells him how disappointed he is in his performance, how he was depending on him to lead the force in sales. The master sales manager can even bring up the closer's family, mentioning how much they are all counting on his performance. For example, he would state that the closer was expected to win a specific sales contract, or attain a certain sales goal. Sales closers cannot dismiss this kind of "talking to"—they are simply too emotionally involved in their work. After this "heart-to-heart" talk is over, all the master sales manager has to do is sit back and watch a sales miracle.

Using Emotions

Ninety-five percent of all sales closers use emotion as their main selling tool when dealing with customers. This being the case, it is no wonder that sales closers are often very emotional individuals. The master sales manager can use these emotions to motivate his closers all season long. Especially during a one-on-one talk, a master sales manager can motivate sales closers by making them cry or laugh, by getting them excited and enthusiastic, or by making them angry. No matter which tactic, or combination of tactics, the master sales manager chooses to execute, the bottom line is that powerful emotions can shake a closer out of a depressed state of low productivity.

TEACHING THE SALES CLOSER ABOUT THE PRODUCT

Each sales closer has to know all the relevant technical and financial details about the product he's selling if he wants to be truly successful. Even somewhat irrelevant information, such as how the product is manufactured, can only bolster the sales staff's confidence.

General Product Knowledge

It is the sales manager's responsibility to educate both his sales force and the sales office staff about the product or products being offered by his company. Another reason why everyone should know this general product knowledge is that it creates a united spirit among all branches of the company. There is a positive, common bond shared by all when, for instance, the advertising division is aware of what the closers are doing and vice versa. Instead of ignorance, all of the different divisions would then respect each other's jobs. Even self-centered closers may find themselves cheering the success scored by the shipping, collection, or manufacturing personnel.

For a sales office to be successful, everyone involved has to be fully sold on the product. A trip to the manufacturing plant, or viewing a company film of a distant plant, would greatly help closers to get enthusiastic about their product, and in turn, they would pass their belief in the product on to the customer. If even one company employee doesn't believe in the worth of the product, then that low grumble could echo and be heard in phone conversations, around new customers, in the mail room or in the restroom. That one complaint about shoddy workmanship, that one beef about overpricing, can undermine the spirit of the whole sales office.

History of the Company

Everyone working in or around the sales office ought to know about their company. This helps them feel they all count, and that they are all an integral cog in the machinery of the company. Even if the company is one hundred years old, the master sales manager has got to create a dynamic spirit among the sales force, as though every employee was an industry pioneer. The people in the sales office, along with the sales closers, need to know how the company functions, who makes out the checks, what is the order of command, what are the company's rules of conduct, who has what responsibility...and so on. Every little detail that can make the employee feel important fosters a staff that is enthusiastic, happy, and prosperous.

Product Benefits

The sales manager regularly has to educate his sales force about all the positive, special features that his company's product has over any of the competition. He has to explain in detail each and every product benefit that a closer might need to get sales. For instance, the closer should be able to convince the customer that someone in their particular position simply must have a cellular phone, with his company's unique range and reliability. As for the product's disadvantages, the closers should know how to counter each weakness by tying it in with a strong point. For example, the closer will defend a top-of-the-line price tag with proof that his (for example) dish washing machine outperforms and outlasts the competition's comparable model.

A thorough knowledge of product benefits entails a comprehensive grasp of the workings of each product being sold. Without asking the closers to be engineers, the manager should make sure that no closer is ignorant of basic operating and construction details. If the commodity for sale is real estate, even a closer who never took geology, should be able to intelligently discuss a plot's superior drainage, and potential for digging deeper foundations. Nothing can salvage the sale of a closer who cannot respond immediately and confidently to that pointed question: "What does YOUR product have to offer that I cannot get at your competitor?"

The Competition

It is just such challenges that force sales closers to know what they are up against. They are often too busy to gather information about the competition, so it's the sales manager's job to inform them. There isn't a sales closer working who couldn't sell a whole lot better if he only knew his competition's product backwards and forwards.

The customer, after all, has often shopped around and knows quite a bit about the pros and cons of competing products. He may have attended demonstrations or heard presentations from competing salesmen. The customer might be carrying a recent consumer guide or company literature listing specific prices and payment plans. It is all too easy for the consumer to wave this literature in front of the closer and "prove" him wrong on some particular details.

The closer who thoroughly knows the competition, on the other hand, can truly impress the comparison shopper who can confirm the closer's expertise: "Yes, Mr. Customer, I read that same consumer magazine which placed our servicing department fourth. If you look two pages later, you'll notice that we had the highest rate of customer satisfaction and that our service department is less emphasized because our equipment so rarely needs servicing. Our competitors use generic, often inferior, spare parts, while we only accept replacement parts from the manufacturer. The facts behind that fourth place standing, you see, only confirm that we are the best."

The Warranties, Guarantees, and Contracts

The sales manager should educate every sales closer on the team on the nuances of the sales contract, especially the warranties or guarantees offered by the company. No closer can reach his full sales potential unless he knows the sales contract inside and out. The master manager makes sure that his sales closers could review the company's sales contract in front of the best lawyers in the land and never stutter, miss a heartbeat, or blink an eye. Sales closers only have to learn their contracts well; it is the managers that have to be able to teach them expertly.

Finances

In the same way that they must be familiar with the sales contract, each closer has got to know the full financial arrangements set up by the company. This includes items like the interest being charged, or the existence of any late payment penalties. The sales manager should hold special seminars for his new closers, and refresher courses for his veterans, to make sure that they have mastered all of the monetary concerns.

The customer often has lots of questions about the fate of his hard-earned dinero. A sales closer who balks at these money questions can be made to look bad and can easily lose a sale. If the closer is stuck in one of these fine points, he should say: "That's an excellent question, sir. Our policy has just undergone some review on that issue, so I'm going to take a moment to consult with management on this one." If the customer is well known to the firm or to the community, the closer might also avoid admitting ignorance by claiming that he is going to ask if an exception can be made in the customer's case: "Let me ask if I can bend the numbers a bit in your favor, given your outstanding credit rating."

Resell or Escape Clause

Each sales closer must also know what reasons or circumstances can allow a customer the right to be released from his contract. A customer who wants to break his agreement must be dealt with fairly. Letting him back out with dignity now will allow him to return at some future time, whereas a customer who has to wrangle with a disappointed closer will be too embarrassed to ever return. Of course, the sales manager should teach every closer the art of keeping his customer in a contract, gently but firmly locking the customer in, so there won't be any fallout or cancellation. There is more on this delicate area in Chapter 6, "Saving Cancellations and Keeping the Sales Process on Track."

TEN SUPERIOR SALES MEETING TECHNIQUES

A master sales manager uses these ten super sales meeting themes and techniques to control, motivate, and inspire all the sales closers he addresses, whether in-house or at a speaking engagement.

1. The "Pre-Qualifying a Customer" Sales Meeting

DEFINITION AND PURPOSE

This is a "shock technique" sales meeting. It is designed to get the absolute attention of every single person in the sales meeting, whether it is attended by twenty people, or an audience of a thousand. In this sales meeting, closers are taught not to pre-qualify customers, not to evaluate them as desirable or undesirable before even saying "hello." This can only be properly executed and delivered if the sales manager or guest speaker is not known to the audience.

HOW IT IS EXECUTED AND DELIVERED

This is a theatrical sales meeting, one that should be rehearsed to get the timing down. Once perfected, the master sales manager will be looking all over his sales region for other places to deliver this high-impact presentation again.

Firstly, the manager or speaker needs someone to introduce him, someone who can be trusted to keep a secret and "play a part" with competence. The second thing that the visiting sales manager or speaker needs is a janitor's large green jump suit, along with a long-handled push broom. After these items have been obtained, the sales manager must brief his trusted liaison who will be doing the introduction, making sure that the whole game plan is understood. Without this person's cooperation this sales meeting's techniques won't work effectively.

While the sales people are filing into the meeting room, the sales manager should slip away and pull the janitor's jump suit over his own dress suit. He should loosen his tie so that it isn't visible behind the overalls, and try his best to look like a janitor doing his work in and around the area of the sales meeting. He should look like he's trying to do a last-minute cleanup job before the sales meeting gets underway.

As the sales people keep coming into the meeting area, the disguised sales manager, pushing his long-handled broom, should try to sit next to some of the best dressed sales people who are settling into their chairs for the meeting. The "janitor" should act as though he's tired, and only wants to sit down and relax for a while. Invariably, the sales people he sits next to will politely tell him that the seats are taken, or they will move away to find other seats. In other words, they tend to think that they are too good to sit next to a janitor when they have come to discuss "big business" and to hear a distinguished professional speaker talk about their highly complex field.

The manager-turned-janitor should move around and try to find a seat in all the different areas of the meeting hall, always playing the annoying role of a nosy custodian who wants to stay for a while to see what is going on and to find out who is going to speak at the podium.

After several attempts to find a seat among the "well-heeled" sales people, the sales manager should go to the very back of the meeting room and stand still while the meeting gets started, waiting for his accomplice to introduce him. The minute he is introduced, he should walk crisply down the center aisle, straight up on the stage, and right to the podium. Without speaking a word during the stunned silence, pierced with the smattering of low, nervous laughter, the speaker should let the push broom fall by the podium, and slowly take off the janitor's jump suit. Slowly, with grand gestures, he straightens his tie, looks at the shocked audience and soberly states: "The reason you don't sell more than you do is because you pre-qualify people, and that is a sales closer's greatest problem."

The speaker delivers these punch lines which rocks the crowd back on their heels: "As a janitor I tried to get a seat in this very room, but I couldn't. It seems that I wasn't good enough for you, or so you prejudged me. If any one of you knew that I was the guest speaker, I could have gotten a seat anywhere. I hope I've proved my point."

Then, after delivering this powerfully demonstrated point, the sales manager should continue on with his prepared talk.

2. The "Countdown-to-Goal" Sales Meeting

DEFINITION AND PURPOSE

Time is the enemy. This is the basic theme in the "countdown-to-goal" sales meeting. The purpose of this kind of sales meeting is to set a short term goal, and to then have everyone in the sales office work toward meeting that one goal on time. The objective here is to create an immediate surge in the spirit of the sales team and office staff. The sales manager uses this kind of sales meeting to start off a two-month sales contest, or to mark the beginning of an important sales deadline.

The sales manager has to keep in mind that he can only use this type of sales meeting three times a year, and that each short term goal has to be just that, short term. Otherwise, the sales closers and the sales office personnel will get burned out early, and will easily fail in the sales manager's total game plan. This short-range "sales contest" is wonderfully devised to get everyone in the sales office to give a one hundred percent effort for an eight-week period of time.

At the end of that eight weeks, rewards, parties, and congratulations will flow in abundance. Individual winners in the competition will be rewarded, but no one should be made to feel a loser. The company has dramatically increased production, so that everyone should be made to feel as if they've won.

Remember, the sales manager has to have set rules for the contest, and strictly follow them. Some closers who worked hard may feel cheated that they did not win in a contest where the supervision was sloppy. If these productive closers perceive that they lost in a competition because it lapsed to a popularity contest, their resentment may carry them right out the door.

HOW IT IS EXECUTED AND DELIVERED

Without anyone knowing, and without any warning at all, the master sales manager (after he has developed all of his plans and knows exactly how his sales contest will work) should announce in one of his regular sales meetings that starting from that very day, and for the next sixty days, there will be an all-out, full-throttle sales contest which requires maximum effort. He should explain that this sixty-day push starts immediately, and reveal the rules of the contest and the rewards waiting at the end of this sixty-day period.

The master sales manager should let it be known that there will be a first, second, and third place prize in the sales contest, and that there also will be a first, second, and third place prize awarded to the sales office personnel who demonstrate the highest efficiency performance during that same period of time.

The master sales manager has got to make large and colorful visual charts and/or graphs to let everyone know exactly where they stand during this sixty-day sales period, and he has to announce the standings each and every day. The master sales manager should make this look and feel like a major horse race. He has to constantly create excitement and enthusiasm. The rewards and/or prizes that the master sales manager dangles in front of his sales troops had better be good ones.

All the master sales manager has to do is raise the price of the product a little during this sixty-day period of time, and that extra money will more than pay for the contest. Remember that this mini-contest will increase sales at least ten percent if done with class.

3. The "Positive Approach" Master Sales Meeting ("Showing Some Class")

DEFINITION AND PURPOSE

In a sales meeting like this one, the master sales manager wants to achieve only one goal, and that one goal will automatically lead to a super day in sales production by his closers.

The master sales manager wants to make his sales closers feel like professional kings. He wants to make them feel that they are on the strongest sales force ever assembled, and that there isn't a sales closer anywhere else in the selling profession powerful enough to climb on board. The master sales manager wants to work on his sales closers' super egos and make them feel taller than they have ever felt before. He wants every one of his men to feel so good about themselves that they will stop worrying about their own personal problems and only focus on the job that needs to be done that day. He tells them how proud he is to be associated with them, and how rare it is for so many "pros" to be on one selling team, all at the same time. The master sales manager can really lay it on thick in a sales meeting like this, because every sales closer there only wants to hear more.

When praising his closers to this extreme degree, the master sales manager had better remember that he can only use this super positive approach once every eight or ten weeks. If he uses it more often than that, it will have no effect at all.

HOW IT IS EXECUTED AND DELIVERED

This sales meeting should be given the day after a good day of sales, NEVER! NEVER! after a bad day, or it will sound too insincere and too phony. After the roll has been taken, the master sales manager should stand in front of his sales force and, without anything in his hands, say something to this effect: "Today I want to tell you all something that I have never before told you as a group. The reason I'm telling you this now is because of something my daughter said to me last night. She asked me how much I enjoyed my job, and after I answered her, she asked me if I had ever told the people I work with how I felt. I thought about that, it bothered me all night. So today, I want to share my feelings with you.

"I have been in this business for a long time, as all of you know, and I have been around many of the best sales closers in the world, at one time or another. But, I want you all to understand something; in all my professional life I have never been associated with so many wonderful and talented people as you. This sales force that we have here is one of the strongest and most powerful sales force that I'll ever have the honor to manage.

"I love my job not because I'm the boss, or simply because it's lucrative. I love it because I can work with you, learn from you, and succeed with you. I just wanted to tell you that today. Now, let's get it all together and have another good day."

After that delivery, the master sales manager should just walk off to his office.

4. The "Bonus Giveaway" Surprise Master Sales Meeting

DEFINITION AND PURPOSE

This sales meeting is unlike the "Countdown-to-Goal" master sales meeting because it's for only one day. This meeting has to be an absolute surprise for everyone on the sales force. It's intended to generate excitement and momentum on the spur of the moment.

The master sales manager has to be on hand all day long (as he should be anyway) to give this "one day" contest the feeling of being official. The master sales manager should know exactly what he wants to accomplish with this contest, and already have the rules written down so that everyone can follow them, and know exactly what to do. The "Bonus Giveaway" surprise sales meeting means just that: at the end of the day (not the next day) the master sales manager must hand out rewards or bonuses to the individual sales closers who make sales.

If that bonus is money, then it's best if the master sales manager hands the winner cash, and has him sign a receipt for it. The reason is simple: cash makes a better impact on the sales force. Sales closers can understand cash a whole lot easier than they can comprehend a piece of paper with someone's signature on it. Remember, cash is green in color, and green means go. Nothing makes a sales closer work harder than to know at the end of the day he can spend his cash reward.

Master sales managers can run little surprise sales contests like this all year long to keep their sales force motivated. It has positive results, as long as their sales closers aren't cheating.

HOW IT IS EXECUTED AND DELIVERED

When sales have been down, and the master sales manager needs to pick them up in a hurry, then this is the right moment for the "Bonus Giveaway" surprise sales meeting. Right after roll call has been taken, the master sales manager should tell his sales force something along these lines:

"Alright, everyone, we all know that our sales have been down, and not what we've projected them to be. Each one of you can do a lot better than you are doing now, we all know that.

"Today we're going to have a little fun, and not worry so much about why we're not selling. So here is what I'm going to do. For every product that you sell today with a full down payment (or whatever stipulations apply), I'm going to give you $____ [fill in the blank] dollars—in cash—before you leave this afternoon!"

At this time the master sales manager needs to hold up a fistful of hundred dollar bills, to let the sales closers know he has the money on hand.

"If you do REAL well, you can have the day off tomorrow," the master sales manager adds with a smile. "This is a one-shot deal, and I hope you take full advantage of it. Now, let's get our act together and start closing like professionals."

After the master sales manager has enthusiastically delivered this little speech, he should let his assistant sales manager take over, and get the sales force geared up for a full day of sales. The master sales manager always has to head the sales force in the right direction, and money always tends to be a pretty reliable compass.

5. The "Negative Approach" Master Sales Meeting

DEFINITION AND PURPOSE

The technique being practiced here is reverse psychology. This is a master sales meeting, conducted by the master sales manager, to make the sales closers feel embarrassed about their performance when they have been selling poorly. This sales meeting is designed to work on the sales closers' raw, "fighting back" emotions, and turn those emotions into positive and productive actions. The master sales manager who gives this kind of sales meeting has to be well respected by his sales closers, or this technique will never work.

The "Negative Approach" sales meeting will produce positive results, but it cannot be used more than two days in a row. Anyone, including the sales closers, can only take so much criticism, and when they have had their fill (when they think that the master sales manager is purposely humiliating them), the closers will rebel, and walk out on the master sales manager altogether, leaving the master sales manager with a sales office and no sales closers. To give a "Negative Approach" sales incentive meeting, the master sales manager must know what he is doing, and he has got to know just how far he can "push" his sales team.

If he doesn't know the limits of his sales force (what they can and can't take), then he should give this kind of meeting in a "watered down" version.

HOW IT IS EXECUTED AND DELIVERED

When the master sales manager's sales team has had four or five days of slow sales production, this is the kind of sales meeting that he can deliver that will produce sales that very same day. Before the master sales manager gives this little talk, he has to stay away from everyone in the sales office (he can even hide away in his private office, with the door locked, if necessary) and give the appearance that he is really upset. He has to give the impression that he is really serious, and he really means business. He can't joke around with anyone, or have any small talk with any of his office staff, before he gives a "Negative Approach" sales meeting, or its effects will be lost.)

When everyone is seated in the meeting room, the master sales manager should slowly walk to the front of the sales group and state:

"There is a reason why I recruited every one of you here to be on our sales team. Remember, I went out of my way to hire you. When you need it, I help take care of your personal problems. I bail you out of trouble. I stand by you, even when no one else would. I believe in you.

"When I hired you, I honestly believed that you were the very best professional sales closers in this country. I expected each one of you to be as good as I have been telling everybody you are. But it looks like that isn't that way. The last four days have proved me dead wrong. I have apparently made a mistake, and now I'm going to have to pay for it.

"Today, I need sales, I don't needs excuses, I don't need any crying. All I need are sales. Today I need a professional sales team that I can depend on, the one I thought I had. I'm under the gun right now, and I need professional performance, not a bunch of babies, or rookies, that I have to tell what to do. Today, I need people who are as good as the ones I have put my money on. Not a bunch of wimps who make excuses because the customer wins and they lose.

"Right now I'm going to go back into my office, and do my job for you, just like I have always done. I'll do that job to the very best of my ability. At the same time, I'm not going to worry about my closers, I'm not going to get all upset and yell; I'm just going to be a professional sales manager, and know that my sales force is out there today being a professional sales team. You expect the best from me, and I give it. I expect the best from you in return. Now, go out there, and show me the professionals that I know I have on this team."

After the master sales manager has made this talk, then he should go right back to his office and shut the door, letting his assistant sales manager get everyone out with the customers. This kind of sales meeting works wonders, but the master sales manager has to deliver it in a very somber and dramatic way.

6. The "Get Off Your Rear End for Money" Master Sales Meeting

DEFINITION AND PURPOSE

The master sales manager gives this sales meeting for one reason only, and that is to illustrate that one has to move to make money. As mentioned earlier, sales closers are generally lazy, and this little meeting technique is designed to cover that "lazy" point. When the master sales manager uses this kind of demonstration on his sales closers, it not only gets results, but it will be remembered and talked about for a long time to come.

This type of sales meeting "trick" might seem elementary and childish to some old pros, but it does make a very basic point. The master sales manager can only use this type of meeting every six months. If he uses it any more frequently than that, it becomes a joke with the sales closers, and its real purpose is simply ignored.

Remember, sales closers are impressed with cash, and this kind of meeting involves cash, so the master sales manager should make sure that he has enough on hand to make this meeting a success. The meeting also requires total secrecy to make a full impact on everyone present. So it's best that the master sales manager execute this sales meeting alone, and not let anyone know his intentions. This is a fun sales meeting, and both the sales force and the master sales manager get an upbeat feeling after it has been held.

HOW IT IS EXECUTED AND DELIVERED

Before anyone else gets to the sales office, the master sales manager has to tape a hundred dollar bill to the underside of every chair that will be used by closers during the morning sales meeting. After he has taped the hundred dollar bills in place, where it can't be seen, he then proceeds on to his regular morning duties, acting as though everything is normal.

When it's time for the master sales manager to give his regular morning briefing, he should only talk about the work habits of professional sales closers. He should stress how necessary it is for closers to always be active, moving over their territories, looking for new customers, and searching for new sales ideas that will improve their sales performance.

Throughout his talk he stresses that movement develops into action, and that no one can make a living by just sitting around the "sales lounge" dreaming. The master sales manager should also stress that sales closers have to hustle, they have to explore new avenues, and they have to dare to believe in taking chances, if they're ever going to get ahead.

After the master sales manager has delivered this speech, and before he adjourns the meeting, he should then instruct the sales closers to all stand up right where they are, and turn over their chairs. When the sales closers discover the hundred dollar bills on the underside, then the master sales manager should say, "Remember, you have to get off your butts to make money."

The master sales manager has made his point about not just sitting around waiting for things to happen, and reinforced the loyalty of his staff. After this type of sales meeting the master sales manager will see a very productive day, and he will easily get back the money he has invested.

7. The "Sharpen Your Ax" Master Sales Meeting

DEFINITION AND PURPOSE

This is a sales meeting where the master sales manager makes a point by telling a story. This story is a great one; it motivates your salespeople to continue learning about their profession. It should be practiced before it is delivered, only because it's too good to mess up in front of a sales force. The point that the master sales manager is making with this story, is how important it is for all of his sales closers to always be learning, and studying new sales ideas and techniques. (Most professional master sales closers think that they know it all and that they can't learn anything new from anyone else.)

The wonderful (wonderful IS the right word) effect that this story has on the sales closers is that it logically gets the master sales manager's point across loud and clear, and at the same time doesn't really put anyone down, or step too hard on anyone's toes. This story, which has to be incorporated into the overall sales meeting theme, works. It will be remembered by the sales closers as making a powerful and fundamental point.

The master sales manager who tells this story will be very satisfied with its results. But, don't forget, this story is to make a specific point, and after that point has been made, the master sales manager should let it soak into the sales closers' minds for a second or two before moving on with the rest of the sales meeting.

HOW IT IS EXECUTED AND DELIVERED

This story can be told at the very beginning of a sales meeting, or sometime during the sales meeting, whenever the master sales manager feels that it will have the most impact. Remember, this is the story that a master sales manager should tell if he wants to make a point about how sales closers need to always study, continually learning new information concerning their profession.

The story: "One time there was this young man from Texas, who wanted more than anything else to be a lumberjack. Now, this young man was big, strong, and powerful. In fact, he could have played on any professional football team, if he was so inclined, but he didn't want that. What he wanted was to live in the northwestern United States and become the greatest lumberjack that ever chopped down a tree.

"Right after he graduated, he got into his pickup truck and headed to the great Northwest. When he got there, he went directly to a logging camp, entered the main office, and told the foreman, "I'm from Texas, and I've driven all this way to become a great lumberjack, so please give me a chance." The foreman thought for a minute and decided, why not? He handed the young man an ax, told him to go put his gear in the bunkhouse, and got him started.

The young Texan went out in the woods, where there were already a hundred other men working, and started to chop down trees. That very first day the young man (to the astonishment of everyone else) chopped down two hundred trees, all by himself. That night he went into the chow hall, had a big meal, and got to bed early, so he could really show everyone his stuff the next day. At dawn he got up, went out, and worked hard for ten hours, but he only chopped down fifty trees. Annoyed with himself (but still amazing the other men), he skipped supper entirely the second night in camp and got to bed real early, determined to do a super job the third day. That third morning he was out in the forest before anyone else, and he worked the whole day plus some, a total of twelve hours, but he only chopped down five trees.

Completely baffled, bewildered, and angry at himself, the young man from Texas slowly walked into the foreman's office and threw his ax on the table, stating, "That's it, I've had enough. I'm not meant to be a lumberjack. I'm going back to Texas." Then he started to walk out the door. That's when the foreman said, "Hold it, young man. You wanted to be the best, well you are. You're the greatest lumberjack we've ever seen around here. Why, you chopped down more trees than ten men put together. But, you've made one little mistake. Every night, after you chopped down so many trees, you forgot to bring your ax in and have it sharpened."

After the master sales manager tells this story, he should then say, "Everyone, just remember, we all have to sharpen our mental axes every single day, if we expect to be the best."

8. The "Disappointment Approach" Master Sales Meeting

DEFINITION AND PURPOSE

This sales meeting is to be used when sales are going badly. This sales is unlike the "Negative Approach" sales meeting in the fact that the master sales manager only works on the sales closers' sensitive emotion of "shame." The word shame stands for a very powerful, and very serious, emotion in all human beings. The dictionary defines the word shame as "a painful feeling of guilt, for improper behavior, or something regrettable, or dishonorable (disgraceful)."

It doesn't matter what anyone says. If a person is shamed, then that person is genuinely hurt. In this kind of sales meeting the master sales manager uses shame to get a positive reaction from his sales force.

The master sales manager had better have the full sales team's respect before he thinks about using this type of sales technique; if he doesn't and uses it anyway, then his whole sales force could rebel, and quit on the spot. This sales meeting is geared to make the sales closers feel bad because they are simply not performing as well as they should be. It lets them know that they are letting down their master sales manager and everyone else in the sales office.

This master sales meeting can't be used more than once every three months because it works on the very raw emotions of sales closers and, heaven knows, closers are super-emotional people. Thus, too much of this kind of emotional rhetoric from the master sales manager would destroy a sales force, instead of moving it in a "positive" direction.

In this sales meeting the master sales manager sticks his neck out, and for five days he has to sell like all the other sales closers, but the results are well worth it.

HOW IT IS EXECUTED AND DELIVERED

When all of the sales closers are seated in the meeting room, the master sales manager should address them in a very serious tone of voice, saying something like: "I have always made certain that I have been associated with the very best sales closers and professional sales managers in the business. Last night, after you all had gone home, I had a private meeting with the president of this company and some of his advisors. They asked me what was wrong with the sales force, why we weren't selling like I had told them we would?

"Well, team, I didn't have an answer. I didn't really know what to say. In other words, I had no excuses. They informed me that if sales didn't get any better, I wouldn't have a job. They gave me only one week to drastically improve the sales situation.

"After the meeting, I went home and looked at my family, the security they have enjoyed by depending on me, and I literally felt like crying.

"Ladies and gentlemen, I truly believe in this company's product that we are selling, and I definitely believe in myself. So, I made a decision last night that I wasn't going to totally depend on you to save my job, but that I'm going to depend on myself. For the next week, until our sales get back to where they're supposed to be, I'm going on the sales line. I'm going to deal with customers myself, personally. I'm going to sell just like I was on the sales force. I'm going to be the sales manager, and I'm going to be a sales closer, both at the same time.

"Why? Because my job, and my family, are worth it. I know I can sell, and I know that I can help get our sales back up to where they should be. If anyone of you want to stand by me, and put out the extra effort that we need, you know I'll be more than grateful. But if some of you think that we, as a team, can't sell anymore, then please quit your job right now. I'm going to make it, with or without you. I'm going to help get sales started again. Let me tell you all one more thing. I always work a lot better knowing that I'm working with true, professional closers standing by my side.

"You now know what I'm going to do, starting today. All I'm asking of you is for you to show me some respect, and tell me what you are going to do starting today."

After the master sales manager has delivered this speech, he should find out what everyone wants to do, then put himself on the sales line and sell his heart out for five days. Sales will go straight up.

> NOTE: *Everyone stays on board. No one wants to quit and miss seeing how good a closer the master sales manager really is.*

9. The "Pen and Pencil" Master Sales Meeting

DEFINITION AND PURPOSE

This master sales meeting is designed to teach each master sales closer a lesson about making decisions. It illustrates the point that when a decision is made, stick with it; don't start second guessing yourself, or become wishy-washy in your attitude. The master sales manager has got to get his sales closers into a confident mental state of mind so that they can make their own sales decisions out in the field; everyday decisions that can be made by sales closers so they won't have to be calling back and forth to the sales office all day long with little problems that they themselves could, and should, solve.

Remember, the more confident a master sales manager's sales closers are, the more they will sell. A professional sales closer should be able to analyze, compute, and diagnose any regular sales problems; then adjust, and make confident, sure-footed decisions to overcome problems without having to always call for help.

If that decision turns out to be the wrong one, then the closer and the master sales manager can get it straightened out together. To have positive and productive sales performances, it's important for the closers to know that they have some say in matters, and that their master sales manager trusts them.

HOW IT IS EXECUTED AND DELIVERED

Keep in mind that this sales meeting exercise is designed to teach and illustrate a point concerning decision making.

After all the sales closers are seated in the meeting room, the master sales manager hands out a blank piece of paper to his team. The master manager then gives the following instructions to his closers: "Ladies and gentlemen, on the piece of paper I just gave you, I want you to write down, in twenty-five words or less, why it is important to always know the latest business trends in our profession. . . . And I don't want you to use your pens or pencils for this task, I want you to use mine."

At this point, the master sales manger shows the group two separate boxes, one containing ink pens for everyone present, the other box holds enough pencils with erasers for all the sales closers. The manager then walks around his squad, offering each closer his or her choice of writing implements.

When all the completed papers have been turned back in, the master sales manager should (in front of the whole sales force) separate the papers written in pen from the ones done in pencil. The master manager should then read the names signed in ink. To everyone's amazement, they will find that the papers filled out in ink belong to the more aggressive sales closers, while the ones written in pencil belong to the weaker, more conservative closers.

From this illustration the master sales manager can explain the difference between the pen and pencil selection: "When you write with a pen, you're not thinking about erasing your promise. When you use a pencil, the thought of erasing your commitment is, subconsciously, always there. It's no wonder that the more conservative closers use pencils, because they subconsciously entertain the idea of a mistake; while the bolder sales closers use ink, which makes their answers more deliberate and decisive."

After the master sales manager has made his point, he should talk about how important it is for sales closers to stand on their own two feet and act with confidence in regard to their everyday sales problems.

(The closers' answers to the question on the pieces of paper don't really matter; all the master sales manager wanted to do was find out who used a pen, and who used a pencil.)

10. The "Razzle Dazzle" Master Sales Meeting

DEFINITION AND PURPOSE

When sales are going well, and everyone in the sales office is in a positive mood, this is the perfect time for the master sales manager to give this type of sales meeting. This sales meeting is designed to keep every sales closer feeling good about himself and his fellow closers, while at the same time keeping spirits high. This sales meeting reflects how positive and pleased the master manager feels about his team.

When giving this kind of sales meeting, the master sales manager must remember to keep control. It's sales meetings like this one that could easily get wild, unless the master sales manager keeps a tight rein on the activities. Don't forget, sales closers like to party and have a good time. (Who doesn't?)

This, of course, isn't all bad. What is bad is when the party starts out for a good reason, then turns around and becomes ugly. That is why it is so very important for the master sales manager to know what he is doing when holding this type of sales meeting. He also has to know how to undo it if the meeting starts to get out of hand.

HOW IT IS EXECUTED AND DELIVERED

The day before this sales meeting is to be held, the master sales manager should announce to everyone that instead of holding the next sales meeting at the usual location, he is going to hold it at a first class local restaurant, where he has already made plans to have breakfast served to everyone present.

The next morning, before the sales closers show up at the restaurant, the master sales manager has the meeting room set up like a banquet hall, with punch bowls full of breakfast juices, and pitchers of spiked drinks.

When the sales closers enter into the "breakfast meeting" area (which should be a place that can be closed off from the rest of the restaurant), the master sales manager greets them, and shows them to their seats like a good host. (The master manager is at the head of the table, of course.) Once the crew has arrived, the master manager invites all present to drink up, relax, and enjoy themselves before the food is served.

The master sales manager should let everyone mingle, for fifteen or twenty minutes. He should then have the sales staff take their seats, while he makes a little speech, where he tells his closers how proud he is of their sales performance, and that this breakfast meeting is just his way of saying thank you for a job well done.

After everyone has applauded him, and the closers are feeling no pain, the master manager should ask if everyone is ready to eat. When all of the sales closers yell, "Yes!" he signals the restaurant manager, who in turn opens up the kitchen doors. In march waiters dressed in formal tuxedos and waitresses in evening gowns to serve the sales closers a fabulous breakfast, presented on silver platters.

In other words, a breakfast fit for a king.

If the master sales manager can afford it, he should also have a lively, upbeat musical group which entertains right through the breakfast party.

Now, the reaction this whole surprise has on the sales closers is simply remarkable. Here the closers are not only being told by the master sales manager how good they are, they are really being treated that way.

All during breakfast, the waiters should handle each sales closer like royalty. After the breakfast is finished, the master sales manager should enthusiastically tell everyone that he expects a great day in sales. Immediately, he turns the meeting over to his assistant sales manager, who gets the closers out of the restaurant and working their customers as soon as possible.

This will be a day when sales production is great. It can be guaranteed. The closers leave the restaurant geared up, excited, and very appreciative.

> NOTE: *The master sales manager has to watch everyone, and make sure people don't drink too much, or behave improperly, as this meeting is the start of a very real business day. That is why control is so important.*

TWENTY CRITICAL NOTES TO REMEMBER WHEN GIVING MASTER SALES MEETINGS

1. Keeping Control

If a master sales manager cannot control his sales staff, then he shouldn't even try to give a sales meeting. The word "control" means that each sales closer has genuine respect for his master sales manager. This means that at the morning sales meeting the closers will sit in a disciplined manner, and let the master sales manager conduct business, without any interference.

Again, the master sales manager gains respect from his sales closers (so that he can enjoy this type of control) by always standing by them, and believing in them. It comes back to being a true leader. No one is going to sit still in a sales meeting and listen to someone talk, if the speaker doesn't know what he is talking about. A master sales manager must speak the truth, and never doubt his own abilities.

Remember, respect is developed through diligence and discipline, and from the repetition of discipline finally comes control.

2. Not Being Late

The sales meeting is the master manager's first line of defense in maintaining control. The master sales manager had better set up a precise time for the daily sales meeting to start, and the staff had better abide by it (himself included), come hell or high water. If a sales closer is going to be late for the morning sales meeting, then he should be required to call in extra early and give the master sales manager, or assistant sales manager, his excuse. If a sales closer shows up late, and didn't have the courtesy to call in, then the master sales manager should lock him out of the meeting room, and only allow him to be the last sales closer given customers to work that day. In other words, put that late sales closer on probation.

> NOTE: *If this type of "customer waiting" situation doesn't exist in the sales company having this morning meeting, then the late sales closer should be fined a cash penalty, or should be required to stay around the sales office all day, but not permitted to work customers (unless, of course, there is some emergency.*

The master sales manager has to be very, very strict in enforcing this fundamental rule. As stated before, all of his basic control methods start with the regular morning sales meeting.

3. Dress Code

If any master sales manager wants to have a successful sales team, he had better pay close attention to how everyone looks. It's a fact of life that if a person is dressed well, he or she will act well. Or, to put it another way, if someone dresses for success, then he will act successful. The master sales manager has to make sure that his sales closers dress professionally while working, so that they will look good in the eyes of the customer.

If a sales closer looks unkempt and sloppy in the morning sales meeting, then the master sales manager had better send him home to change, immediately. There should be no excuses whatsoever for looking unprofessional.

If a closer keeps looking bad, the master sales manager should either advise him on his wardrobe, or fire him.

4. No Phone Calls

When a master sales manager is holding a sales meeting, it has to be absolutely understood by every one of the sales closers that no one may receive any personal phone calls. The only exceptions should be legitimate emergencies. (Business calls are not verboten.)

The reason for this strict rule is so the master sales manager can conduct a serious meeting. Sales closers have to learn, through daily mental exercise if necessary, that when their master sales manager talks, everyone listens. The master sales manager has to drill into his people a subconscious awareness that he rules the nest. Every little incident that the master sales manager tolerates will only erode his leadership capabilities and the respect the sales closers hold for him.

If the master sales manager lets one tiny thing slide, that will pave the way for other things to slip by, thus creating an avalanche that will eventually bury the master sales manager.

5. Don't Tell All

It is very important to remember that if a master sales manager tells his sales staff everything that is going on in his sales office (bank business, contract negotiations, meetings with lawyers, company programs for future product development, delicate mergers, and financial transactions), he will lose his job. Every bit of inappropriate information that he passes out will come back to haunt him, until he finally quits his job, or gets fired.

The professional master sales manager cannot, repeat CANNOT, tell all things to all people. He has to hold the details of his sales game plan in his hands only, and no one else's. If he lets other people know his "secret" plans and courses of action before they are actually carried out, there will always be somebody (or a bunch of somebodies) who will try to interfere, derail, sabotage, or distort his good intentions.

6. *Fifty Minutes Only*

If a master sales manager holds his regularly scheduled sales meeting any longer than fifty minutes, then he's passed right by the sales closers' "maximum time limit" for concentrated attention. (This fifty minute "time limit" does not apply to sales meetings which are held as training classes and learning sessions. This "time limit" is applicable only toward the regularly held sales meetings.)

Master sales closers are a restless breed, revving to succeed early into each new day. If a master sales manager talks too long, or is long-winded while explaining certain points during his sales meeting, his audience will get bored, and what he is saying won't have any impact on his sales closers.

The sales closers want "energy charged" sales meetings to help pump them up for the day. The master sales manager can only deliver this energy in short, powerful blasts, not as an ongoing stream of dialogue.

7. *The "Sidekick" Master Sales Manager*

The master sales manager has got to use his "Sidekick" sales manager all of the time, at every sales meeting. The reason: it's the "Sidekick" sales manager who helps make the master sales manager look good, and stay important. The master sales manager has to remember that he can't do everything by himself, and his "Sidekick" sales manager is there to help.

In everyday sales meetings, the master sales manager doesn't always have to tend to the trivial matters; it's the "Sidekick" sales manager who loyally organizes the details. Being that a good "Sidekick" sales manager is a responsible human being, he can take attendence, make inventory adjustments, give out general information to the sales force, or tape those hundred dollar bills to the bottom of the sales team's chairs.

There are numerous important duties that can be delegated to the "Sidekick" sales manager. The master sales manager should be more than grateful for this comrade-in-arms.

NOTE: Sales closers like to know that their master sales manager is thinking of them, so it's a very good idea for the master sales manager to call roll himself every now and then.

8. Mixing Closers and Managers

When the master sales manager has team captains, or assistant sales managers, in addition to his trusty "Sidekick" sales manager, he had better make sure that the assistant managers sit right in among the sales closers. The master sales manager wants more than anything to create a total team spirit, not one that is divided between closers and managers.

If there is such a division on a sales force, and all the managers sit up front, at a table facing the sales closers, who in turn are facing them, a friction develops, and the gap that opens between these two "parties" will be awful. Team spirit will be divided. The "two parties" will learn only to console and trust themselves, and that grand sales production plan simply won't work.

Don't forget that there should always be a feeling of helping and caring for each other, and a common goal of succeeding. This is how a professional sales team should act, day in and day out.

9. Explain Goals

The master sales manager has to let everyone on the sales force know what their company's goals are for the selling season. The master manager has to clue everyone in on both the short-range goals and the long-range goals. That way the sales force can mentally visualize the exact same target and share the same enthusiastic spirit, a united spirit directed toward a common goal.

Without this unity of thought and spirit, a sales team is not a force (concentrated energy that creates action), but merely a bunch of individual sales closers, frantically running in every direction, bumping and stumbling over each other's paths, hoping to accomplish a miracle.

Remember, a football team works together to win; it's that simple.

10. *Give Recognition*

When a master sales closer does a good job, then by all means give him positive, sincere recognition at the morning sales meeting, right in front of everyone. Don't ever delay rewarding a closer for an outstanding performance. Sales closers thrive on being known for their professional sales talent. It's the most wonderful music to their ears to hear their master sales manager congratulate them for a job well done.

The master sales manager should use his sales meetings like an actor uses the stage, to create excitement, jolt emotions, expand feelings, and develop character. He can accomplish all of these fantastic goals by giving out praise to the master sales closers who deserve it.

Remember, if you hand someone a trophy, they won't ever let it get tarnished.

11. *Embarrassment*

When the master sales manager is holding one of his sales meetings, and a sales closer asks him a question that he can't or doesn't want to answer right then and there, the manager must remember not to get ruffled, frustrated, or embarrassed. The master sales manager must always keep his composure, above all other things.

A master sales manager must always appear calm, and appear that he has everything under control. No closer alive will ever have any respect for his leader, if that leader gets all shaken up over mere words.

When asked a question that needs to be dodged, the master sales manager should tell the closer making the query that he'll answer them later when more facts are in, or that he'll be happy to discuss it in private.

Don't forget, the master sales manager has to stay in control.

12. Outside Disturbance

If something unexpected happens during a sales meeting, like an irate customer comes barging into the sales office demanding his money back, or the local vending truck backs into the side of someone's car, then the master sales manager must stay perfectly calm. Let him dispatch the "Sidekick" sales manager to tend to the problem and report back.

Never should the master sales manager interrupt his own sales meeting to go see what has happened himself. The reason: he has to put himself above being "normally inquisitive," like everyone else, and stand firm (confident), keeping his attention focused on the matters at hand.

A master sales manager must continually be a sound example for his sales closers, displaying calmness, rather than getting all rattled, when an unexpected event occurs.

Don't forget, the master sales manager is the general of his army, and he can't fall to pieces in front of his men, or he'll upset the whole team.

A leader is a leader by example.

13. Keep Records

It's very important for the master sales manager to keep minutes of every sales meeting. The reason is simply to protect himself. For instance, if the sales closers complain, and say that this or that was going to take place at a certain time, and it never came about, then the master sales manager is well protected. All he has to do is refer back to the minutes of the meeting where the disputed subject was discussed, and then immediately solve the controversy by showing the sales closers precisely what took place and exactly what was said.

It is also important for the master sales manager to keep daily accounts of his sales closer's selling percentages, length of time spent with a customer, cancellations, and any other important data, so he knows the exact performance record of every person on his sales team.

14. Cliques Do Exist

The master sales manager has to understand that there will always be "cliques," buddies who stick together, in every sales force. It doesn't matter if some of them are in management and some are sales closers; friends will be friends. The master sales manager should never try to break up one of these close-knit groups; he won't succeed, and he'll be resented by everyone involved.

Cliques are very good for the sales force, because within their own sphere, the members help each other by supplying support and encouragement in ways master sales managers and outsiders cannot.

The only thing that a master sales manager has to watch out for are groups that cause negative thinking within the sales force. If the master sales manager finds such a case, then he should have a talk with the leader (there always is one), and get things straightened out. If the leader is hard to manage, then the master manager should fire him, and let him be an example to the other clique members. They, in turn, will either shape up or ship out.

15. Use Teams

To create temporary excitement and "playful" competition, the master sales manager might want to divide his sales force into "positive rivaling" sales teams.

In this type of inter-sales force competition, each team has its own colors, names, and team captains. This kind of game playing has its positive points. A team effort will last for a short while, not a full year, because the sales closers simply get burned out on this elementary sales psychology.

Don't forget that sales closers will start mingling with one another after a while, and forget that they are supposed to be on opposite sides during the sales team competition period. And the more they socialize with each other, the less they care about whose team is ahead or behind in the competition. Soon the master sales manager's great "team competition" idea turns into a great fizzle.

Remember, sales teams are good for only short periods of time.

16. The "Sidekick" Manager's Ego

The master sales manager has to be constantly aware of the attitudes that his "Sidekick" manager and his assistant sales managers project.

It is very easy, and dangerous, for an assistant sales manager to develop a "big head," and think that he is something really special. Many assistant sales managers and team captains have destroyed an entire sales force because of their egos, and their "mightier than thou" attitude.

If the master sales manager discovers this negative attitude creeping into an assistant manager's mind, then he should immediately get that manager alone, and they should have a very serious talk in order to straighten him out. The master sales manager has to kill this horrible "ego" disease before it gets out of control and destroys the sales force.

17. A.M. Is Better

The best time of day to hold master sales meetings is always in the morning hours: seven-thirty or eight o'clock. The sales closers are more alert and energetic at this time of day.

The master sales manager's main objective in having early morning sales meetings is to get the sales closers psyched up for their first sales call. The master sales manager knows that if his sales closers do a good job of selling their first customers, then the rest of the day should follow suit.

Remember, nothing breeds success like success. The master sales manager has to be the sales closers' alarm clock, morning news informer, rear end kicker, and cheerleader...every single day, IF he wants a successful sales force.

18. Hangovers

When the master sales manager looks out over his sales closers at his morning meeting, and he sees that several of his men are barely able to hold their heads up because of a hangover, or late-night party, he should feel no pity for them.

Coldly, the master sales manager should simply ask the sales closers if they are capable of selling anything today. (They will automatically answer in the affirmative.) He should make sure that the closers are presentable to the customers. Then he should continue with his normal agenda, and not mention the subject again.

If a master sales manager shows no mercy, and acts as though everything is alright, then the sales closers with the hangovers will feel obligated to sell something to prove themselves. Plus, they will feel so physically and mentally bad, knowing that they have to actually work the entire day, that there is a good chance that they won't come to work in that beat-up condition again.

19. Stay Around

To have a successful sales force, the master sales manager has got to be around the sales office all day long. He can't just give a blockbuster sales meeting in the morning, and then leave the office, expecting his assistants to carry the day.

A master sales manager has to stay on board. He is the leader, and while he is at the sales office his men will work. Once he is away from his sales office, his men will play. This is a universally known fact. Sales closers have to be watched, pampered, and led, if the master sales manager wants to have a winning sales record.

The master sales manager cannot give direction to his men when he isn't there to guide them. Long hours are only part of a master sales manager's job, but the rewards are great. Sales closers will only work as hard as their master sales manager works. This is a proven fact, and every master sales manager alive had better understand it.

> NOTE: *Remember that while in the sales office, the master sales manager has to be highly visible—not behind closed doors in his private office. His closers want to be recognized, and they can't if he can't see them.*

20. The Sales Team

The master sales manager has got to understand the stone cold fact that his sales force will only be as good and as powerful as he is.

If a master sales manager is weak, wishy-washy, uncertain of his actions, or disloyal, then his sales team will act the same way. The master sales manager is the only leader of his sales team. It is his lone responsibility to make his sales team successful, not only financially, but morally as well.

The master sales manager is the pulse of his sales force, and he cannot ever afford to forget it. He has to get to work earlier, and stay at the office later than anyone else. He has to keep calm, be in control, and stay aware of everything that goes on, all the time.

By the way, that doesn't include teaching and managing sales, projecting future sales goals, and being an honorable and courageous gentleman. Needless to say, being a professional master sales manager is not easy. Aside from all of these qualities and efforts just mentioned, if a master sales manager wants a strong and powerful sales force, then he, himself, must be strong and powerful. He must remain that way, even when all others fall short, or retire from exhaustion.

CHAPTER 4

Helping the Sales Team Win: How the Sales Manager "T.O.s" Customers

A "T.O." situation is where a master sales manager truly gets to demonstrate his sales prowess. A "T.O." in sales means a "takeover" or "turnover." This grand event takes place when the master sales manager is called in by his closer to finalize a sale or sell the difficult customer. The premier topic in this section is the sales manager's personal attitude toward "T.O.ing."

THE MASTER SALES MANAGER
AND THE "T.O." SITUATION

The master sales manager has three perspectives from which he develops a winning attitude toward his "T.O." involvements. The manager must proceed:

       a. Constructively
       b. Egotistically
       c. Subtly

Additionally, the professional sales manager must be a sales closer at heart. He should love it when he is asked to "T.O." one of his sales closer's customers—it's like old times for him. No matter how long a master sales manager has been away from selling his own customers, he never forgets the excitement and the positive energy that flows through everyone at the closing table when a customer finally makes the buying decision to purchase the product. So, it is these well-honed instincts and fond memories in his mind that spark the master manager's enthusiasm when he is asked to "T.O." His attitude toward a "T.O." situation is not only that of job responsibility, but one of true delight.

In a take over sales situation, the master manager gets the chance to not only sell the customer, and look good in front of all the other sales closers, but for that short time he's back in the trenches, on the closing table with the chance to be a sales closer again. No true sales manager wants to pass up an opportunity to get in the spotlight and shine. If he successfully "T.O.s" that difficult customer, he accomplishes more for team morale than a dozen seminars or sales meetings.

The Constructive Approach

The sales manager's first priority must be sales. Because his very career depends on it, he should be eager to help his sales closers out in any tough "T.O." situation that arises. The master sales manager does not take a single customer for granted. When a sales closer asks a master sales manager to "come in" and help him nail down a deal, the master sales manager should feel honored.

A manager cannot think of a "T.O." situation as a waste of his valuable time or a nuisance on the part of an incompetent closer. The master manager must remember that when a professional sales closer can't finish off the job that he is paid to perform, he reluctantly swallows his pride when he asks for assistance. The sales manager should secretly feel pretty good, if not downright excited, when the closers respectfully look to him to make the difficult "T.O." Though the manager might be tired, or mentally exhausted at the time, he must remember that he is the leader of the team, and any "T.O." request should give him an instant surge of sales energy, as it will give him the opportunity to switch modes and use his sales expertise.

No matter what his mood, the manager must never humiliate the closer at this vulnerable time. He should step up to the closing table to greet the closer and customer with a brisk step and a genuine, ready smile.

With all three parties present, the manager should ask the sales closer to inform him as to what has been covered. The master manager should then turn to the customer and ask him what are his questions and/or hesitations about purchasing the product. When he has obtained this information, the master manager must mentally process it, noting where the customer's apprehensions lie. Using some of the many skills he has honed over the years, the master sales manager waylays the customer's fears, designing a purchase plan that suits the customer's needs. During this presentation, the master manager looks to his sales closer for support, but he must also have the insight to spot the various points that the sales closer may have overlooked. By clarifying murky areas and using his years of acquired wisdom, the master manager should thus be able to succeed in his sale, teaching the closer the fine points of closing a deal in the process.

When the papers have been signed, everybody has won. The customer is satisfied, the master sales manager has triumphed in a potentially difficult situation, and the sales closer has learned how to better handle a potentially difficult customer.

The key to the constructive approach is that the sales closer benefits not only financially, but mentally as well.

The Egotistical Approach

The master sales manager who takes an egotistical approach toward handling a sale will close the deal purely for the satisfaction of achieving what the sales closer perceived as being impossible. When the sales closer calls on the manager to get a problem customer to consent to the deal, the sales manager must effectively use all of the panache and charm he has developed in his many years of sales. Beaming with excitement, and the pride that comes with expertise, the master sales manager confidently comes to the closing table and takes the spotlight, literally pushing the closer to one side. The master manager establishes his relationship with the customer, making the client the center of attention. With insight, knowledge, a pat on the back, and a ready smile, the master sales managers placates any of the customer's purchasing fears. Displaying his confident competence and expertise on the product, the master manager makes the customer understand why he needs this product. Thus, the customer consents to the sale.

To succeed in the face of skepticism makes the master manager feel great. The master sales manager in a "T.O." situation is egotistic in the sense that he, himself, likes to know that he still has the skill and talent to step over to the closing table and get a reluctant customer to sign on the dotted line. When a master manager knows in his own heart that he still has that wonderful gift, then he can pretty much take care of his other sales office responsibilities without too many problems. He will then feel like a master sales manager to himself and to his admiring staff.

The Subtle Approach

A master sales manager has never lost the sales closers' most subtle techniques. And when it comes time to "T.O." a customer, the master sales manager will use every legal, persuasive technique available to get the customer to buy.

Here's an important warning: It's all too easy for a sales manager in a "T.O." situation to be caught not practicing what he preaches. Some sales managers tell their closers not to use too much high pressure when selling, when at the moment of truth, the manager will use more high pressure than any five sales closer put together.

Now, there is a great temptation for a sales manager to use "gray area" selling tricks when "T.O.ing" a closer's customer. After all, he doesn't want to look bad in front of his sales team by missing the customer and not getting a sale. Most sales managers feel that when they are called in to "T.O.," they should demonstrate skills in getting the sale. They will only accept defeat if it's a matter of finances on the customer's part. A lot of master sales managers will therefore bend more than one rule to sign up a customer, rather than lose face in front of the sales closers by letting the customer "win," and walk out of the sales office without a contract. The master sales manager knows that he might buckle under pressure on such occasions and end up undermining his own sales principles. He must try his best to overcome this pressure and to score his knockout punch according to the rules.

WHEN IS THE RIGHT TIME FOR THE MASTER SALES MANAGER TO "T.O."?

It is very important for the sales manager to know exactly when to "T.O." if he hasn't been invited to the closing table. If a sales manager doesn't understand the difference between good timing and bad timing, then he should never try to "T.O." A professional "take over" or "tactical offensive" can only be successful if the sales manager knows perfectly well what he is doing. Always remember that timing, and gauging a customer's emotions are everything when it comes to executing a professional "T.O."

When the Closer Is Losing the Customer

Since sales are the bottom line, the master sales manager doesn't wait to tell a closer what he might have done to save a lost sale. When a master sales manager sees that one of his sales closers is losing a customer's interest and enthusiasm for the product, then he has the full right to step in on the sales presentation and give all he's got to save the deal. If the sales manager steps on the sales closer's toes, well then, that's just too bad. It has to be remembered that the customer is everything. If there is any outside chance to satisfy the customer and make a sale, then it's worth the risk of making a closer feel temporarily slighted. The master sales manager does not stand by and watch a valuable customer slip through the fingers of a sales closer who has given up on the customer too early in the presentation, or who has not taken the time to completely explain the product.

Of course, a manager who bursts into the scene should do so with all of the charm he can muster. After a "T.O.," he should soothe the closer's bruised ego by congratulating him on their winning "team" effort. When the closer is feeling good, the manager can then slip in a few words of advice on how to better handle a similar situation in the future.

When a Closer Asks for Help

The sales manager has a professional responsibility to his closer, and should be as available as possible for a "T.O." when they need one. The sales manager has hired and trained his closers, and for him not to follow up and help his people sell when they need him is nothing short of abandonment.

Of course, a manager shouldn't go to the other extreme and be a meddler. The master sales manager should strike the right balance by knowing the staff well and by rushing over to fledgling closers only when they're losing altitude fast. The sales closers will do their own closing, but they are sure to produce a lot better knowing that they have a strong and powerful backup system waiting for them in the sales office, if they should need it.

> *NOTE: You may get a sales closer who has gotten into the habit of calling on the manager to "T.O." every one of his customers. He's using the sales manager as a crutch. This will only keep the closer as a dependent cripple, hobbling over the manager's busy schedule. The master sales manager, in this situation, has the full right to ignore this type of sales closer's distress calls. He may want to slowly wean this closer away from the dependency with increasing unavailability, or increasingly early exits from the closing table—which force the closer to execute more and more of the actual closing process.*

When the "T.O." Has Been Prearranged

When selling a customer, a master sales closer has many sales techniques and closing methods at his disposal. One of the very basic (and oldest) techniques is the "good guy vs. bad guy" sales scenario. In this dramatic duet, the sales closer can play the good guy or the bad guy. In either case, it has been established in advance, that when the sales closer reaches a certain point in his pitch, the master sales manager will interrupt the sales meeting. If the sales closer has taken the good guy roll, the master manager will come to the table *pretending* to "defend" the customer. The master manager will say something like, "Look, can't you see the customer doesn't want the product, why are you pressuring him to buy it?"

The sales closer will retort with a comment on how the product will enhance the customer's life, and he's only looking out for the best interest of the customer.

Then the master manager will "offend" the customer by saying, "Obviously, Mr. Customer is not out for his own best interest. He is comfortable with his way of doing things, and doesn't have the desire to keep up with today's technology."

As the master manager and the closer banter back and forth, the "good guy" closer "defends" the customer by explaining how the product will better his life. The "bad guy" manager subtly belittles the customer because of his hesitancy about making the purchase. Remarks about technology, and that the customer obviously does not wish to benefit his life, work particularly well. If the customer comes to his own defense, which he most likely will, then he has convinced himself to buy the product.

This prearranged "T.O." is an extremely effective way to get a reluctant customer to commit to purchasing the product, and it makes the closers realize the benefits of having a sales-wizened veteran on their side.

When the Master Sales Manager Knows the Customer

Occasionally a situation arises when a sales closer's customer is a personal friend or acquaintance of the sales manager. The sales manager might also have a "referral customer" who comes asking for him at the sale office by way of one of the manager's past customers. It might even be a customer from the sales manager's recent past as a sales closer. When situations like these occur, then it is proper for the manager to "take over" this customer, since it was really "his" in the first place. The customer, in fact, might well feel slighted if the friendly, familiar face he came looking for is not willing to see him.

In these cases, the master manager should not take the commission. He should either divide it up as a sales bonus for the whole sales team to share, or he should give it to the sales closer who first encountered the customer. If a sales manager does take the commission himself, it can be guaranteed that problems will develop from jealous closers, even though the master manager may have earned the commission. The petty office gossip could well escalate into nasty little rumors, and the commission check will never be worth more than a pile of regret. There are times like these, when a master sales manager knows that earning respect—and avoiding thin-skinned ego bruising—is much more valuable than earning money.

When the Closer and the Customer Don't Understand Each Other

When a master sales manager surveys the sales pit or watches his salespeople on the lot, he'll sometimes notice that the closer and the customer aren't really communicating. They are simply not understanding each other, and the closer doesn't realize that he's not connecting. This is when the sales manager should think up a good reason to introduce himself into the sales presentation. The master sales manager knows all too well how valuable customers are, and he doesn't want even one of them to get away.

A communication problem with a customer is a green light for the sales manager to step in. Not only can he possibly salvage an unlikely sale, but at the same time he can give the sales closer some valuable instruction. If he pays attention, the closer can learn some selling points from the master, and determine where he got off track with his customer.

When the Master Sales Manager
Wants to Make a Point

One of the main responsibilities that a master sales manager has is to constantly teach and train his sales closers in the delicate art of selling. This sales training exercise is an ongoing affair that doesn't end with classroom lectures and simulations. If a master sales manager sees one of his sales closers making a basic mistake while attending his customer—a mistake that could very well lose him the sale—then a master sales manager will immediately step in and "take over." The master sales manager will not only avoid embarrassing the closer, but will try to make his "T.O." feel spontaneous and natural. (Only after the customer is gone will the master manager spell out to the closer what he did wrong.)

When this action is taken by the sales manager, the sale closer should stay put and try to learn a few things. The closer should never ask the manager if he's done something wrong within earshot of his customer. This makes the closer sound like an amateur and the company seem like a training school.

When to Wield Authority

Sometimes a sales closer will have a customer who won't do any business with anyone but the boss. A professional salesperson knows that the "let me see your supervisor" line is some customer's way of intimidating the closer and getting—or so they think—better attention and better deals. This "hardball" playing customer causes problems for some rookie closers; or for those closers who might take it personally, get upset, and lose control in such circumstances.

The master sales manager should step right in, and utilize all of the authority and sales material he needs to "T.O." and sell this crusty kind of customer. The sales manager should also reassure the salesperson, with visible pats on the shoulder that signal to all present, that the closer remains trusted and valued. The battle-wise veteran manager knows that this customer has no problem with the closer, other than the fact that he was dealing with "merely" a salesperson. This "legend in his own mind" thinks that only the top man can deal with a client of his high caliber.

It is therefore essential that the manager who steps into one of these situations does so with an air of complete authority, which almost verges on arrogance. The master manager must be more than a match for the confrontational air of this kind of customer. Even if it's not his style, this is the time for a master manager to swagger, bark commands, dominate the conversation and turn on his laser-powered eye contact.

The master manager's sales technique is what the customer asked for, and that's what the manager should deliver in spades. Nine out of ten times—as with so many bullies—the skeptical, contentious lion will turn into a pliant lamb when confronted with an even greater master of control and intimidation.

Should the sales manager approach this type of customer with a soft passivity and quiet eagerness to be of service, then both the closer and the manager will come off as wimps and losers. Nice guys do close sales, but when the customer is an arrogant son of a gun, such nice guys will not finish at all.

When the Master Manager Needs Sales

There are times in every sales manager's professional life when his sales closers are slumping and the sales figures for the division are dropping. This is the time for a true master sales manager to roll up his sleeves and start working directly with the customers, even if some of his sales closers feel as though he's intruded upon their domain. Somebody has got to get the job done, and at bleak moments like these, the master sales manager should feel that he must personally leap into the trenches and lead the charge. When the sales manager starts moving around from customer to customer, interjecting his positive input and experience, his sales closer will usually get energized as well. In a few hours, sales production often starts turning around for the better.

Action speaks louder than pep talks from the sidelines. Don't forget that the sales manager is the definite leader of this sales team, and when that team is tiring, or starting to sputter, it is the master sales manager who had better step in and take the lead.

When a "T.O." Needs a "T.O."

Many times the closers will call a well-qualified assistant sales manager in to "T.O." their customers, or they'll ask for the assistance of the "Sidekick" sales manager. Even this is as it should be, because a master sales manager can't be everywhere at once. These assistant sales managers are trained for just such service, and they also should be closers at heart.

But, as with a lot of well-made plans, sometimes things don't go as well as expected. Often the same problem that prompted a sales closer to call in an assistant sales manager for a "T.O." is just too tough to handle. The assistant sales manager may well need help on a difficult question, or dealing with a tough personality. It is then time to call in the master sales manager to save the whole mess.

When a situation like this occurs, the assistant sales manager should introduce the manager to the customer, explaining the problem so that everyone understands the situation, then excuse himself. The assistant manager should leave the customer with he original sales closer and the sales manager.

NOTE: *Never should the sales closer, the assistant manager, and the sales manager all try to sell one customer simultaneously. The customer will not only become very nervous, but he will feel like the sales team is ganging up on him, plus he'll become confused. And no customer will buy a product if he or she is confused.*

WHEN IS THE WRONG TIME FOR THE MASTER SALES MANAGER TO "T.O."?

Just as knowing when to take over a sale is a delicate art to master, it is equally as important for a sales manager to know when not to "T.O." The wrong timing, the wrong tone of voice, or the wrong strategy on the sales manager's part could kill a sale faster than someone throwing ice water in the customer's face. Every master sales manager who runs a winning sales force must instinctively know when to stay out of a closer/customer relationship. It might appear that negotiations are breaking down, but the intelligent sales manager knows to stay away from the closing table when a closer is actually setting up the customer for an effective climax. If need be, closer and manager should develop signals to prevent an unnecessary "T.O." that could prove to be counterproductive.

Both the use of signals, and the art of noninterference, have a parallel in baseball management. A successful manager will not interfere with a pitcher who seems to be missing the strike zone, but who is actually setting up the batter for his "out" pitch. If the manager yanks the pitcher for a relief man—a baseball "T.O."—he might end up doing more harm than good for his team.

When the Closer and Customer Have a Good Rapport

The master sales manager never interferes with a sales closer who has already built up a relationship with a particular customer. The master manager knows that his sales closer is constantly developing a feeling of trust during his sales presentation, creating a common bond with his customer. The sales manager who intervenes without invitation could very well disrupt the closer's delicate, trusting rapport with the customer. The master sales manager can smell the difference between an undeveloped sales close (which still has much potential) and a closer-customer relationship that has derailed and needs his saving grace.

When the Customer Is Silently Thinking to Himself

When a sales closer has his customer in the final closing stages of his sales presentation, the customer might spend some time silently contemplating whether or not to purchase the product. This contemplation period, or silent review of notes and figures, might only take half a minute, but it feels like an eternity to the more impatient closers and managers. At this special time, when the customer has asked for his solemn moment of decision, do not, for heaven's sake, interfere.

When things are quiet, Mr. Sales Manager, don't touch! Keep still and let the sales closer complete the transaction in good time. No news is not necessarily bad news, and an attempted "T.O." during these sensitive seconds is likely to backfire.

Don't forget that the sales closer has worked for quite a while to get the customer in a positive buying mood. All it takes to break this "fragile spell" is one wrong word or an inappropriate move on the part of a manager with good intentions. A master sales manager knows that the difference between nipping a "no" in the bud and annoying a customer who is quietly mulling over his tally sheet and sorting things out in his mind. In a situation like this, the manager should go ahead and let his sales closers sell, giving his trained professionals the benefit of the doubt until they actually hear the customer balk.

When the Customer Is Rude

A sales closer may occasionally get a customer who is extremely rude and hostile. Neither the closer nor the manager is trained in psychology, so there is absolutely no reason for the manager to go in and attempt a "T.O."

There is no sales matter involved when a customer turns to loud, accusatory, or vulgar language. The customer already has a big chip on his shoulder, a chip that even a master sales closer couldn't remove. This customer will only get more angry and more arrogant when the sales closer brings in another person who represents authority. Some of these more disturbed customers will only think that the closer and his reinforcement (the manager) are ganging up on him to further humiliate him for not being able to afford the product. The customer will only increase hostility toward any entering sales manager, causing everyone more problems than a potential sale is worth.

The sales manager should just let the closer try to calm this kind of customer down, making sure that the customer is quietly escorted out of the sales office before he disrupts sales production for everyone.

When the Closer Lies to His Customer

A sales manager has two primary professional responsibilities to the company he works for. He has to both present his company in a positive light, and protect his company's reputation. With this professional code of honor in mind, the master sales manager will not allow any of his sales closers to misrepresent his company, or it's products, or lie to any of the company's customers.

Now, if a sales manager finds one of his closers lying to a customer, then the master sales manager will have a serious meeting with the offender. The manager should give him one more chance or fire him on the spot—so that the other closers get the message. If a sales closer lies to a customer, and the sales manager backs him up (supports the lie), then they both should be fired.

A master sales manager will not "T.O." for a lying closer under any circumstances. He doesn't even want to appear as though he's supporting a lying closer. The master sales manager knows that the customer, his company, and his self-respect are to good to be soiled by a dirty lie.

When the Closer and the Master Sales Manager Don't Have Their Stories Together

The sales manager and his sales team have got to use the exact same facts and sales information when discussing their company's products with the customer. (Otherwise, honest mistakes and discrepancies will sound like lies and deception.) The sales manager in a "T.O." situation cannot be saying one thing to the customer when the sales closer has said something completely different just minutes before. The sales closer and manager must coordinate their facts and figures to keep customers from getting confused or downright angry.

> NOTE: *Whenever there is updated sales information, the master sales manager should not merely rely on memos or brief announcements at sales meetings. The masterful manager will drill his closers over and over again, until the new product information is completely mastered. This prevents those damaging discrepancies and keeps the staff selling in harmony, and with complete confidence. The manager might even hold a "game show" meeting with a desirable prize to motivate the staff to know those new facts and figures cold.*

When a Closer Needs to Stand on His Own

Some sales closers use their sales manager to close their customers so often that they have gotten into the very bad habit of relying on their manager to actually sell the customer for them. These sales closers literally use their managers as a crutch. This awful habit can destroy a sales closer, as he begins to lose his sales sharpness. Without the ability to close customers on his own, he turns into a mere order taker.

It is up to the master sales manager to prevent this from happening to any of his valuable sales closers. If the closer needs this crutch for more than the first several weeks, then perhaps it's time for him or her to limp away to some other firm. The master sales manager will zealously protect his sales closer's special talents, and never let his selling gifts turn soft from lack of use.

When the Master Sales Manager
Is in No Shape to "T.O."

It's a sad point to bring up, but there are times when alcohol might prevent the manager from performing his professional duties. When a sales manager has partied too much the night before, and is nursing a hangover, or still smelling like booze, then he shouldn't even think about going in and "T.O.ing" a sales closer's customer. Not only will he wind up missing the sale, insulting the customer, and embarrassing the closer, but he will be setting a poor example of leadership for everyone in the sales office. And believe you me, no one will forget it if the boss makes a fool of himself.

The master sales manager is on stage all of the time; his people look to him for guidance and inspiration. It is one thing if the manager comes in with a bad cold, or even a bit groggy on medication. But it is quite another thing when his minor incapacity is alcohol-related.

> NOTE: *Whenever the manager feels he might not display behavior that is up to the level of a true gentleman and leader, then he is hurting, rather than helping, the company by coming into work.*

When the Closer Is in Full Control

When the sales manager observes that one of his sales closers is in complete control of his sales presentation, then he should just lay low and not get involved. The worst thing that a sales manager could possibly do is stick his nose into a well-oiled sales presentation that is still in progress. The intrusion is unwise because it could only cause unnecessary questions and confusion on the customer's part. The customer is likely to think that something complicated or conspiratorial is going on, that the manager is getting into "the act" because something is not right. This kind of thinking on the customer's part can be quite damaging to the sales closer.

Remember, even a friendly interruption on the manager's part can compromise the sales closer's timing and sense of control. So, keep hands off when there's no problem to correct. If the sales closer needs the manager later on during the "sales closing period," then you can rest assured that he will call out loud and clear.

When the Closer Has Made an Enemy

When a sales closer has inadvertently upset his customer and made him very angry during the sales presentation, the master sales manager should fight the temptation to play policeman and just stay away. One must give the customer time and room to cool off—even if the manager is convinced that his closer was at fault. The sales manager would only be adding fuel to the fire if he tried to step in and resolve things while the customer was raging.

The sales closers are professionals, and if they can't calm down their own customer enough to at least get him out of the sales office, then it would be even more difficult for a perfect stranger (the sales manager) to try and do so. In a problem situation like this, or when the disgruntled customer sits back down at the closing table, rather than leaving, a sales manager might signal for the closer to leave the room. Outside, beyond the angry customer's violated "space," the manager could brief the closer and coach him on some quick crisis management.

When the Sales Manager Is Not Prepared

Nothing could be worse for a professional sales closer than to call in his manager for a "T.O." on his customer, and discover that the boss does not have all of the necessary facts to go ahead and close the customer. Prior to calling the manager, the closer has built up his manager's reputation to the customer, then he brings him in for the clincher. When the manager can't come through with the goods, the closer's bubble is burst, and the sale is in deep trouble.

How does a nightmare scenario like this come to be? For example, the manager may know the general figures, but doesn't exactly know how to calculate the payments according to the given specifications of the customer. Or, the sales manager may not know how a new product's warranty really works, or he can't find some important production information that the customer wants. Any one of these panicky scenes could kill a sale for the sales closer, because the tension and delicate timing of the "T.O." close magnifies any error into a catastrophe.

The master sales manager must therefore be fully prepared to field any and all of the customer's questions and objections. That is his job. No manager becomes a master sales manager if he is too lazy to go out of his way to learn about his product. If he thinks that he already knows everything there is to know, and that charisma, without homework, will bring success, then he doesn't belong in the sales profession. To "T.O." a customer professionally, the sales manager has to be ready both mentally and psychologically. Like the "fireman" of the pitching staff on a major league club, the competent "T.O." man is the firm's M.V.P. He must always be able to bail out his team of sales closers in a pinch.

THE DELICATE ART OF "T.O.ING": HOW TO "TAKE OVER" AND SELL A SALES CLOSER'S CUSTOMER

Every sales company needs a master sales manager to ensure maximum sales. Not only is the manager supposed to make sure that his sales closers do their job of selling customers, but he is also supposed to roll up his sleeves and actually help them. That is what the "T.O.'s" are all about. Remember that the initials "T.O." form the acronym for both "turn over" and "take over." This means that the sales closer either turns his customer over to his sales manager to get a sale, or his manager decides to come in and take over his closer's customer to accomplish the very same purpose.

Remember, when a sales manager "T.O.s" a customer, he is after the close that will get the customer to sign the sales contract. It is this delicate "T.O." operation that is going to be discussed on the pages ahead. Closing a customer is not a game to be taken lightly, as an ego trip or an exercise in persuasiveness. Closing a deal is very serious business, it involves real money, and the transaction is made with a living, breathing, feeling human being.

Special Notes Regarding Customers

Remember that customers are only people. They are not monsters who can destroy you in two minutes, and they are not saints who are incapable of doing any wrong. Customers are simply human beings like ourselves, with varying talents and feelings. They want only two things in life—besides a good deal on your company's product—to be loved, and to be respected. To be a true master sales manager, you should give out an abundance of these two basic wants to everyone you meet. If you have a good supply of these precious commodities, share; customers, closers, acquaintances, and family will make you feel great in return.

A master sales manager can treat every customer he "T.O.s" as though that customer were the only client he was going to have all year long. With that kind of intense caring showered on the grateful customer, a master manager's net closing percentage will consistently approach a whopping eighty percent!

Putting it another way, the sales manager must take the time to understand each one of his closers' customers and to empathize with their particular problems. He should patiently probe their doubts and questions, and then tell the customers the honest truth about owning and financing his product. Done with a caring and enthusiastic presentation, he will sell ninety percent of the folks he talks to. The ten percent that won't buy from him will likely be those customers who simply couldn't afford the product.

Remember, even customers who appear rude, moody, greedy, crude or arrogant still want to be treated well and respected. Now, it's tougher to project warmth to such people, but they all can be sold, if they are treated properly. Because they are used to harsh treatment from authorities, they will be especially affected, even touched, by a manager's caring. They are most likely testing you, daring you to hate them. If you project love and understanding, they might be worth a half dozen "easier" customers in their ultimately warm response to you.

> NOTE: *Love is far from the whole story here. The master sales manager also uses an array of learned sales techniques, several secret psychological methods and various tricks and traps— not to cheat or scam the customer, but to point him or her to the place where the advantages of owning the product are more clearly seen.*

Know for a fact, customers don't mind a hard, or even an aggressive sell, just as long as they are treated with caring respect while being sold. Once again, customers can't be lumped into easy types and categories. No matter what their exterior, they're all good old human beings. As you learn more strategies, never lose sight of the love and respect for the customer that must back up and rival all other learned techniques.

Setting the Stage for a "T.O." Operation

Before the "take over" or "turn over" is discussed, the stage has to be set so that you, the potential master sales person, can envision the overall environment and atmosphere in which a "T.O." operation takes place.

> NOTE: *Sales offices all differ. Some use phone rooms or have sales closers working all across a certain state or territory. They might use individual sales offices or closing rooms. For this illustration, however, picture a single sales office with one central sales area, as in a car dealership. This sales area setting (closing room) could be large enough to hold anywhere from twenty to two hundred pairs of sales closers and their customers. Size doesn't really matter, it's the environment and the atmosphere that counts. It should be an energy-charged room, surrounded by walls decorated with product information, sales reports, brochures, product pictures, and every other imaginable thing that could help the sales closers sell.*

This central sales area (the "sales pit" or "closing room") is where all the sales closers bring their customers to go over final product and purchasing details after they have presented or demonstrated their company's product. This is where the closer proceeds to ask the customers to buy their product.

It's in this exciting setting that the professional sales manager stands back, out of everyone's way, while constantly watching all the activity that is taking place on the sales floor. It's here that the sales manager waits with "restless patience" (like an actor whose stomach is full of butterflies before going on stage) for one of his sales closers to come up and ask him for help selling his customer. Or, on the other hand, here is where the sales manager enthusiastically waits for one of his sales closers to raise his hand from the closing table, indicating that the closer needs help with his customer.

This is the setting that the reader should envision as he reads the details about how a master sales manager "T.O.s" one of his sales closer's customers, aiming to get the customer to sign the sales contract right then and there.

The following illustration and guidelines will take you, step by serious step, through an entire "take over" operation so that you can experience and learn the masterful "T.O." methods without any confusion or difficulty. The following illustration is written in a no-nonsense manner, and if the reader carefully follows the guidelines then he or she could start "T.O.ing" sales closers' customers immediately.

> NOTE: The instructions here are not carved in stone. Anything can happen during a "T.O." situation, and the master sales manager will be able to adjust to the unexpected circumstances. When faced with these little crises, a sales manager must not get thrown off guard, or lose his composure.

The happiest reason for not following the given steps for a "T.O." or other close is when the customer says he's ready to buy the product the second the sales manager sits down at the closing table. Forget the protocol and all of my advice. Take down that order right then and there. There will be many times when a sales manager is "T.O.ing" that he'll have to throw the rule book out of the window and just fly by the seat of his pants. If you are the type that must only live by the book, then get out of sales and become a C.P.A.

The Drama

The master sales manager knows that there are three major acts in the "T.O.ing" drama:

Act I: *The Approach.* When a sales closer is sitting with his customer at the closing table, and he has been unable to get his customer to make a buying decision, there are several unobtrusive ways to call in the master sales manager for help:

1. The sales closer should matter-of-factly tell his customer that he should get further clarification on the product and that it would be helpful if the sales manager would clarify things from a different perspective. Explain that the added help will be to the customer's advantage.
2. Wait for a complex question and let the sales closer cheerfully announce that he'll ask his master manager to come in and respond.
3. The sales closer could tell his customer that he doesn't have the authority to act on the customer's request. His inquiry deserves to be considered, so it's time to go talk to the sales manager.

Any and all of these little excuses will work for the sales closer, but the closer has to control his customers and make sure that they don't simply walk away when the closer is out getting the master sales manager. A professional closer will act with the necessary tact and speed to bring the master manager into the scene.

This is when the master manager makes his approach. The sales closer and the customer are already seated. Cheerfully and confidently, the master manager strides up to the table and joins the negotiations.

Act II: *The Close.* Once everyone is comfortably seated, the sales manager gets all pertinent information from the sales closer about his customer's problem. The sales manager plans his primary game plan based on the circumstances, and his assessment of the customer. Implementing whichever "T.O." techniques are necessary, the master sales manager calls on his years of acquired knowledge and skill to seal the deal and have the customer sign the contract.

Act III: *The Exit.* Once the customer has signed on the dotted line, the sales manager graciously excuses himself and exits the scene. The "deal" is done, and the manager leaves the sales closer alone with his customer to tie up all the little loose ends.

Now, these are the three major steps that have to be taken, in exact order, for the sales manager to productively "T.O." But within each major step, there are three important substeps that also have to be executed well for the professional "T.O." to really work. These essential additional steps will be explained to the readers as they appear in the following "T.O." illustrations.

IMPORTANT SALES AND PSYCHOLOGICAL MATTERS TO KEEP IN MIND WHEN "T.O.ING" A CUSTOMER

Watch the Sales Area

The master sales manager is a leader. He's the boss of the sales office, and it is his responsibility to know everything that is going on all around him. He has to be acutely aware of everyone's responsibilities and performance in the sales office, especially in the sales area. The master manager does some of his own snooping around, and has some staff intelligence gathering, to help him maintain complete control.

When a sales room is really buzzing with energy, with closers and customers talking, squawking, cussing and discussing, there had better be someone on top, in complete control. It doesn't matter if it's a "boiler room" full of people on the phone, or a car lot with customers and closers chasing each other—there had better be that one individual who knows all the parts of the puzzle and how they are placed together to make the whole day, week, month, year totally successful, regarding maximum sales performance.

The Problem Solver

The sales manager who is called in to "T.O." a closer's customer is being looked up to as the problem solver. He is seen as the one person who can help him sell his customer and get him down "on paper" (convincing him to sign the contract). The customer is also expecting much out of the manager in this situation. He sees the manager as the only person with enough authority and know-how to take him into purchasing the product with confidence.

A master sales manager who is asked to go in and "T.O." had better understand these perceptions in the minds of the sales closer and customer, and he had better act, if necessary, to satisfy those perceptions. He should straighten his tie, lower his voice and play the part that is envisioned and expected of him. He has to go in on a "T.O." looking, acting, and sounding like someone who makes the final decision around the sales office. He shouldn't know the meaning of "maybe" or "I think." If he addresses any customer with an attitude of weakness or an inflection of self-doubt, then the sale is in deep trouble.

In other words, the master sales manager is the answer man. If there is a problem, both the sales closer and the customer should feel confident that the person they are talking to will find instant solutions to even complex questions.

The Nervous Customer

The master sales manager never forgets that when he is called in to "T.O." a closer's customer, that customer is either edgy and scared, or pugnacious. That is why it is so very important for the sales manager to radiate a quiet authority that won't challenge or intimidate the customer. The master sales manager gives the customer time to mentally adjust to him and his added presence at the closing table. The customer has got to calm down and relax, knowing that this "T.O." man isn't the big, bad bully he anticipated.

If a sales manager just walks up to the customer to "T.O." and immediately bangs away at his sales closing "pitch" (without so much as a "How-de-do?"), he will kill that sale faster than a customer can jump up from the closing table and run out the door.

Listen to the Customer

When a master sales manager goes in for a "T.O.," he had better first be quiet and listen to the customer describe his difficulty with the product you are attempting to sell. It's crucial that the sales manager hear the whole story, and not assume what the customer is saying, or cut him short. Even if he's heard the customer's rap a thousand times before, a master manager will appear interested and respectful. Remember, the manager was called in to solve a problem, not to rudely and impatiently preempt one. To fully comprehend the situation in personalized detail, the manager should hear the customer out. The "T.O." situation is not the last minute before the buzzer; it's a time to finesse points rather than to bust in for a "slam dunk."

Don't forget that customers are not stupid. They can see in the sales manager's eyes whether he really cares or whether he only sees checks and commissions. A man's eyes tell all, they can't lie. A manager can't just hide behind a smooth voice and a firm handshake. Genuine respect and concern must radiate from his eyes, the windows of his soul.

Be Authoritative but Humble

The master sales manager acts like a true leader when he goes to a closing table to "T.O." He has to project an air of authority at the same time that he is being decent and humble. He cannot go into a "T.O." situation with an attitude that radiates a snobbish and egotistical "I-know-it-all" personality. Many customers will not put up with some wise guy sales manager who is trying to show off his "closing" ability and sales techniques to the whole office. If the customers don't walk out insulted, they might play the game for a half hour and then refuse to sign.

On the other hand, even customers who despise the carnival barker's hard sell expect the "T.O." man (the sales manager) to be a strong and powerful individual. Their expectations are linked to the manager's title and their special situation. The master sales manager will pleasantly surprise the customer by conforming to their authoritative vision of him, but also displaying kindness and genuine consideration for the customer.

Tell a Background Story

When the master sales manager first meets the customer in this high-pressure role of being a closer for a closer (at the "T.O.") he should break the ice and the tension during the beginning of his "warm up." He should tell the customer some personal anecdote or otherwise introduce some non-threatening conversation designed to relax the customer. For example, "I noticed your school ring. I've got an embarrassing story to tell you about my own school ring. . ." This story could be something about the manager's family or job, anything intimate. This pleasant distraction must be a sincere gesture of friendliness that can't be taken as a phony ploy.

The customer has to have a friendly feeling towards the sales manager, or there may never be a sale in the pressured ambience of a "T.O." situation. Everyone prefers to do business with a friend, and the easiest way to make a friend out of a stranger is to share some personal information that creates an immediate bond.

Kick the Closer

When the sales closer asks his sales manager to sit down at the closing table with his customer for a "T.O.," the spotlight and microphone switches from the closer to the manager. From the moment the master sales manager is introduced to the customer, the sales closer should sit perfectly still and pay "respectful" attention to the master sales manager. The obedient closer should politely confirm his sales manager's statements with an affirmative nod of the head, and speak only when spoken to.

> NOTE: *If the sales closer is jeopardizing hundreds or thousands of dollars because he wants to get his two cents in, the sales manager should either kick the closer under the sales table, or shoot him a "Shut Your Mouth!" look.*

The closer must not throw the manager off at a time like this. He should only continue to be involved if he and the manager have a dialogue planned out for the occasion.

The customer, too, can get confused when both the closer and the manager are trying to sell the same product with their own separate styles and perspectives. A confused customer is rarely a buying one.

Keep Everyone Involved

When the sales manager sits down at the closing table with the sales closer and several people who make up the customer's party, he had better have enough sense to keep everyone present involved in the goings on. The master sales manager never leaves anyone out of the conversation, whether it's the spouse or the second cousin of the principle client. He knows that invariably the one left out will feel somewhat hostile, and they could turn into the opposition element that kills the sale.

The master sales manager also knows that winning over a spouse or a child can turn the tide of a buying decision with a reluctant client. Remember, everyone sitting around the closing table helps make the buying decision—even if they don't have speaking parts in the drama.

Don't Use the Term "Finance Man"

The sales manager must train his sales closers not to introduce him to customers as the "finance man"—even though motive for the "T.O." may be a financial matter. The customer will only prejudge such a person to be just another high pressure sales closer, coming in to hit him on the head with a bigger hammer. The sales closer should tell his customers that the man they are about to meet is the boss, the sales manager. This sounds a lot more impressive than someone called the "finance man" or "finance manager."

Don't Tell the Closer's Weakness

After a sales manager has "T.O.ed" a closer's customer (whether the sale was made or not), the temptation is to publicly tell the closer (in hearing of his colleagues) what went wrong with his particular sales presentation. The sales manager is always the teacher, but a public lesson is a form of punishment, not education. The master manager has a very real responsibility toward criticizing sales performances, but only in private. A valuable public lesson can be made at the next day's meeting, with the identifying facts left out.

The confidential, student-teacher relationship is compromised with any public critique, and the master manager should realize that even mild humiliation could be counterproductive.

No sales closer will function well if he lacks self-confidence. And self-confidence will be hard to come by when the whole sales force knows about the closer's weaknesses and mistakes.

Divorce That Extra Couple

When called in to "T.O. where a sales closer's customer has friends with him (as opposed to members of the immediate family), the manager should try to get rid of the tag-along pals. The manager should tell the "extras" that he will be discussing personal financial matters, and graciously invite the guests to the lobby area for some coffee. The master sales manager will be polite, but firm, in his request. He knows that the tag-alongs can only be trouble: most couples won't buy if their friends oppose it.

The manager's line about respecting private financial information is not just a line. Many couples will feel extra pressure when discussing finances in front of friends, and uncomfortable customers will either not buy, or will buy and then have to cancel (when their friends aren't around).

Don't Jump Around

The master sales manager never jumps from one closing table to another, juggling customers as though they were bowling pins. Customers want to feel unique and important, and they don't want to see the distinguished manager, who has come over to see them, rushing off like a chicken with its head cut off. Customers are always watching what goes on; they are more observant and sensitive than many closers and managers realize. The "T.O." situation only heightens this sensitivity. If treated like numbers, and not individual human beings, customers won't let the sales staff achieve their quotas.

Know the Closer's Habits

The professional sales manager should know the selling procedures and closing habits of each of his sales closers. This can be learned by simple observation over a period of time—four weeks or twenty-five customers (whichever comes first). Besides coordinating facts, as discussed above, the "T.O." artist should effect a harmonious transition from the closer's sales presentation to his own managerial close. Styles should not be so jarringly different that a customer feels confused.

Let Your Face Be Known

Whenever possible, the master sales manager makes a point of saying hello to every single customer who comes into his sales office. This preconditions every customer, allowing them to get used to his face. This way, should the master manager be called in to "T.O." a closer's customer, he won't be a threatening stranger who has arrived out of nowhere.

The sales manager doesn't have to stand at the front door of his sales office to accomplish this pre-conditioning "ritual," he can politely introduce himself at the appropriate moment when customers and closer are paired off.

> NOTE: *This is a good tip to remember. When greeting the customer, the master sales manager should use the word "today." For example, "How are you today, Mr. Customer." This word "today" will subconsciously stick in the customer's mind, letting him know that all sales procedures are designed for "today"—to do business today, not tomorrow.*

Be Yourself

The "T.O." situation can be awkward, and a sales manager who tries to put on an act only makes things worse. Nothing turns everyone off more than the manager trying to break the ice by telling a joke he can't deliver properly. The master sales manager should just be himself, never doubting his own unique personality.

If the sales closer's customer needs some warming up or relaxing, then the sales manager should ask some friendly background questions rather than attempting to entertain. Whenever a manager puts on a mask, it soon starts to peel and the truth begins to show.

Train Assistants to "T.O."

The sales manager has a professional responsibility to train his assistant sales managers in the fine art of "T.O.ing." It is his obligation to his company to teach his people everything he knows, so that they, in turn, can help and teach others. The master sales manager understands that to be successful, he has to surround himself with successful people. There is a temptation to remain the only person in the office who can handle a "T.O.," but what's good for the ego is bad for the sales team.

Don't Lose Your Composure

Whether the action at the closing table is good, bad, or ugly, the master sales manager should not get emotional or blow his top. He has to keep his composure under every kind of unforeseen circumstance. If he doesn't, then everyone around him will surely fall to pieces. He is the captain of the ship, and the one everyone else turns to when a storm kicks up.

If a sales manager loses his temper and throws a childish fit, he is giving the rest of the sales office the right to do the same. With all eyes on the sales manager, it is also likely that everyone's respect for him will plummet.

Working the "T.O." pressure table is bound to result in some nerve-fraying situations, and an occasional insensitive remark by the customer. Instead of throwing back a provocation or insult, the manager should politely excuse himself from the closing table and stay away from the customer. It's a lot smarter to lose this one sale than to lose a whole room full of sales when a shouting match breaks out.

Don't Clutter the Closing Table

When a sales manager goes to a closing table to "T.O.," he had better make sure that his entire work area is neat and uncluttered. It turns off many customers to see chaos overflowing from their would-be answer man; plus all of those sets of sales pamphlets, working papers, charts, or company brochures could distract the customer and reveal some troublesome questions.

What greater nightmare can there be than the customer eyeballing your old sales brochure, or one from your competition (which shows lower prices than you are now offering)?

Would you buy from a man who takes ten minutes of fumbling to find the right price table, form, or contract? Try to be as well organized as possible, and inspect closers periodically for similar desktop disasters.

Know Your Manners

Here's some serious advice for managers, even if you think some customers don't "deserve" more dignified behavior: always conduct yourself like a gentleman or lady in and around the sales office. There is no place for foul language or uncouth behavior at this position, no matter how well it played with your buddies back in your closer days. Chances are that some higher-up, catching you spitting tobacco or using "America's noun or verb," may put you right back down where you started. A master sales manager is the dignified leader and representative of his sales force and sales office. Even the toughest blue collar customers respect his qualities. He is treated—and paid—like a gentleman because he knows how to reflect success, prosperity, and class.

Critique Every Sales Closer

It's the sales manager's full right, obligation and responsibility to develop every sales closer on his sales force into the very best professional salesperson possible. It's only fitting then for the sales manager to pull a sales closer aside, and to discuss, in a constructive manner, what he did right or wrong in his recent presentation. The sales closers will only learn and improve if someone cares enough to teach them in the field, above and beyond previous classes or seminars. And this responsibility, of course, lies with the master sales manager.

CHAPTER 5

The Five Deadly "T.O." Closes

S tuck with an adamant or confused customer? These "power closes" are a master sales manager's secret weapon for succeeding against all odds. Learn them and learn them well, for these five "T.O." sales closes are a master manager's key to success, as skill and knowledge are what set the master sales manager apart from the more menial members of the sales pack.

Remember: A "T.O." close is only a planned maneuver in which the master sales manager puts the customer into a position where he, or she, can make an intelligent buying decision.

THE "YOU'RE NOT APPROVED" CLOSE

This "T.O." close is designed to put the customer on the defense, using the science of reverse psychology to play on a customer's ego. It will definitely get some reaction from the customer, one way or the other.

This "T.O." close will make the customer feel that he is not qualified to own the product. The master sales manager who uses this "T.O." close had better be a good actor, and he had better be ready for an argument.

How to Use the
"You're Not Approved" Close

When a sales closer is getting nowhere with an apathetic, rude, or arrogant customer, it is a good time to call his manager in for this "T.O." After the sales manager confirms the customer's problem, in this case his attitude, the master sales manager may want to try the "You're Not Approved" "T.O." close.

To implement this high-impact procedure, the master manager meets briefly at the closing table with the closer and the customer. He then excuses himself from the group, and disappears into his office. Two minutes later he reappears with a serious and downcast air about him. Solemnly, the master manager takes his place at the table and declares, "Mr. Customer (use their first name, if possible), I've got some disturbing news for you. Please forgive me and the company for wasting your time here today. Just now, when I went back into my office, I checked out your credit rating on our computer. Your current financial condition isn't quite strong enough to enable you to purchase our product under our present purchase agreement.

"Mr. Customer, I'm sorry that we didn't catch this earlier, we could have saved you the time you've spent here. I really do apologize, and we really wish that you could have enjoyed the ownership of our product."

Immediately after this shock to the customer's ego is delivered, the sales manager casually turns to the closer and sighs, "Well, Mr. Closer, you tried your best. These are really nice people you have here, but I don't think there is anything the company can do to help complete the sale in this case."

In the next pause, the stunned and insulted customer is likely to attack the bad credit remark and challenge the sales manager on his subtly condescending put-down. The sales manager should act like he is on the side of the customer, and say that he will be glad to check with the source of his information to confirm that it is indeed correct.

The angry customer, at this point, will be upset about this disclosure of his confidential credit rating. The more the customer talks, the more ammunition he is giving the sales manger in his battle to discover and break down the customer's true purchasing objections.

When the real objections come out, the sales manager should go ahead and overcome them. He should then say how much he admires and appreciates the customer, no matter what the computer seems to say. The manager gets up and declares that he will personally see to it that finances don't stand in the way of the customer owning the product. He should then stick out his hand for the customer to shake, acknowledging that the sale has been made.

THE "DID THE CLOSER LIE?" CLOSE

This is a "T.O." close that has to be rehearsed between the sales closer and his manager before the closer connects with his customer. This "T.O." close can be quite effective, but it has to be acted out by closer and sales manager with complete credibility. If, for one second, the customer thinks this "T.O." close is a "put on," the sale is lost for sure. In this unconventional "T.O." close, the customer is not the party under the gun, he is backed into the close in the role of the witness. The customer doesn't find himself in the middle of a close until it is way too late.

How to Use the
"Did the Closer Lie?" Close

When the customer keeps refusing to close a deal and sign a contract, the sales closer should excuse himself from the closing table to go get his sales manager for this prearranged "T.O." strategy. When the sale closer comes back to the closing table with his manager, and all the introductions and explanations have been made, the sales manager should turn to his sales closer and ask him the following questions, in a tone so pointed, that the customer will feel like nobody remembers that he exists:

"Let me ask you, Mr. Closer, did you tell Mr. Customer about the special options on our product."

"Yes sir," comes the closer's obedient reply.

"Did you, Mr. Closer, explain to Mr. Customer everything about our special warranty?"

"Yes, sir," protests the closer, vulnerably he looks to the customer for confirmation and support.

"Did you, Mr. Closer, take the time to show Mr. Customer the special advantages of owning our product?"

"Why, yes, sir, I certainly did."

The customer may start nodding his head and trying to support the beleaguered closer, who is now getting lectured at the customer's expense.

"Did you tell Mr. Customer about our financial setup and contract arrangements?"

"Yes, sir...I'm sure if you asked him..."

At this point the customer should be ready to defend the poor closer, as he should be feeling quite guilty that the sales closer is in trouble.

"Did you also discuss with Mr. Customer our company's reputation, and its past performance history?"

"Yes, sir, I honestly did. You wouldn't have been ashamed of me if you were here listening to my meeting with Mr. Customer."

"Speaking of honesty, Mr. Closer, did you lie to Mr. Customer about anything? Is that why Mr. Customer has been holding back from making a purchase?"

"Oh, no, sir, I assure you that I didn't," the closer responds, humbly.

The sales manager, acting satisfied with the sales closer's answers, should wait a dramatic few seconds, and then turn straight to the customer and demand, "Well then, Mr. Customer, why didn't you buy?"

BOOM! Direct hit! The customer has been feeling empathy for the poor closer and now he's sitting there with his mouth half open in surprise, not knowing quite how to respond. Off balance as he is, he will likely stammer out some kind of excuse as to why he didn't buy, or come out and give the real reason for not purchasing.

Once a master sales manager hears either the customer's lame excuse or true objection, he should go ahead and overcome it—leading right to a sale.

> NOTE: This kind of "T.O." close operation is not only fun, it's very effective. The customer has been set up and forced to admit that either he can't afford the product, or that there is no good reason why he doesn't go ahead with the purchase.

THE "BOARD OF NAILS" CLOSE

This is a story close that illustrates to the customer in a simple way how he or she has lost sight of their goals in life due to the wear and tear of daily pressures. This "T.O" close will work wonders if it is told in a soft, sincere voice by the master sales manager, and, of course, properly adjusted to the product being sold.

How to Use the "Board of Nails" Close

Say, for example, a closer is trying to sell time sharing or insurance to a reluctant customer. When the customer won't budge and shows no positive signs of moving toward a sale, this is a perfect time for the master sales manager to use this emotional, logical "T.O." story close.

With the customer and closer sitting at the closing table, all attention is trained toward the master sales manager, who should say the following: "Mr. Customer, let me tell you a story. There was this man having coffee one morning in his own kitchen, minding his own business, when his wife walks in, and suddenly, out of nowhere, says to him, 'You know, you're mean to me, you treat me badly and say nasty things to me.'

"The husband looks up from the breakfast table and says, 'What? What do you mean?' The wife explains, 'You have been mean to me all this past year, and I'll prove it. I'm going to put a plywood board on our kitchen wall, and every time you're mean to me this next year I'm going to hammer a nail into the board. I'll show you just how hateful you are.'

"Well, the husband just shrugged his shoulders in a way that said, 'Okay, whatever' and ignored his wife, thinking she was just upset that particular morning. In no time a year passed, and again the husband is having his morning coffee in the kitchen. His wife enters, points toward the board on the kitchen wall and says, 'Look at that board. I told you you were mean to me.' The husband looks up, studies the board and sees nothing but solid nails. Even on the edge there are nails. The board couldn't hold another nail, and it must weigh 600 pounds. The husband suddenly realizes that his wife was—is—telling the truth, and he says, 'You know, you're right. I have been mean to you. I'll tell you what I'm going to do. This next year, to make it up to you, I'm going to be especially nice to you. And every time I am, I'm going to take one of those nails out of that board.'

"The wife agrees, and the subject is dropped. One year later the husband is sitting in his kitchen, proud as punch, waiting for his wife to enter. She comes in for her coffee, and he says triumphantly, 'Look at that board now. There is not a single nail in it. See, I told you this past year I was going to change.' The wife looks at the board, and sure enough, all the nails are gone. But then she points to the board and says, 'Yes, that's true, all the nails are gone. But just look at that board!'

"As he looks, he sees a board that is full of old nail holes and claw hammer marks, where he pulled nails out. There are scars where bent nails had once been. The board is nothing but a warped and mangled piece of wood. The wife says, 'You see, the nails are gone, but the scars are still there.'

"Well, Mr. Customer, I'm telling you that you don't have to live like that anymore. You don't have to keep looking at nothing but scars and lost dreams. With my product you can have some of those dreams back. You can have what you've always wanted.

That, Mr. Customer, is what my product can do for you."

After the master sales manager tells this story, he should give the customer a minute to let it sink in. He then should say, "Mr. Customer, I need your name right here" (on the contract). The sales manager should immediately stick out his hand for the customer to shake in agreement. This story close will work miracles, but it has to be told with sincerity and emotion. The customer must feel the sales manager is on his side—making a genuine illustration of the customer's own needs and wishes.

THE "YOU BELIEVED" CLOSE

The "You Believed" close is designed to get the customer thinking about how his decision not to buy is foolish. This "T.O." close will make the customer think to himself that maybe he is being silly by waiting to buy the product at a later date. The sales manager must convince him that there is no benefit whatever in waiting, and that any delay is merely due to his nervousness about having to make a buying decision. This "T.O." close will work, but the master sales manager has to deliver this "T.O." message with sincerity, logic and calm, so that the customer gets the point first time around. The manager must convince the customer that erring on the side of caution is still erring—in this particular case.

How to Use the
"You Believed" Close

First, we must set the stage for this "T.O." close. In this illustration we'll use a customer who has to make a buying decision at a real estate development. The customer has been invited to the resort for a three-day and two-nights-free vacation in which he is obligated to take a tour of the property with a real estate sales closer.

This "You Believed" close is a wonderful close to get the customer on the closing table who is interested but is scared of making the big decision (to buy into the resort). The master sales manager should say the following: "Mr. Customer, let me ask you something. When you got my company's invitation to visit our resort, you believed that we would honor that invitation, didn't you? Sure you did, because you're here now, aren't you? [Note: Always give the customer a second to agree, then move on.] And after you drove your family two hundred miles to visit us, you believed that we would actually have accommodations for you in one of our advertised condominiums, didn't you? Then, when you checked into the condominium, you knew it would be fully furnished, down to the color TV and kitchen utensils we promised, didn't you? And you also believed that we had golf courses, swimming pools, horseback riding and other activities like we said, didn't you? And is it not true, Mr. Customer, that all these things were here as advertised? Well, you were also told that you would be given a tour of our resort by a salesperson, whom you have met, and you know that this was true too.

"Mr. Customer, you believed everything we told you about us and now you're actually here. Everything we told you and advertised was true, correct? Well, then, let me ask you this. If you believed everything we've promised so far, and everything we've said has come true, then why don't you trust us the rest of the way, and know that we are going to stand by all of our financial obligations to you? You know, you remind me of a champion swimmer who swims halfway across the lake and then says to himself that he can't make it. So he turns around and swims all the way back to shore. Now does that make sense to you? Of course not.

"All I'm asking you to do is believe us the rest of the way. You've believed us so far, so don't doubt yourself and don't doubt us now. Mr. Customer, I need your name right here (on the contract) next to mine." At this time the master sales manager should either stick out his hand for an agreement or give his pen to the customer to sign the contract. This "T.O." close is powerful if delivered in a tone of sincerity and confidence.

THE "YOU CAN AFFORD IT" CLOSE

The "You Can Afford It" close is the simplest, most understandable and powerful "T.O." close there is for its particular purpose. This "T.O." close will get a sale or get action from the customer every time, if used at the right time and in the right circumstances.

This "T.O." close is designed to work on a customer who wants the product, but who keeps telling the closer or sales manager that he can't afford it at this time. This close is so simple and potent that all other sales books completely overlook it. This down-to-earth "T.O." close can't be praised enough.

How to Use the
"You Can Afford It" Close

When a customer says to the sales manager that he likes the product but can't afford it at this particular time, the master sales manager should quickly reply, "Mr. Customer, I know you like my product, and I know you'd like to own the product. Let's just see if you really can afford it." (Note: The sales manager or closer had better be close enough to the customer to freely discuss personal finances. If this closeness or trust doesn't exist, then this "T.O." close won't work very well.)

At this time the master sales manager should get a blank sheet of paper, the back of a contract order sheet or worksheet, and say to the customer, "All right, Mr. Customer, let's put down in black-and-white your monthly expenses. Let's see for sure if you really can't afford the product. (Note: At this moment, before the master sales manager starts to reckon the customer's monthly bills, the manager must secretly jot down his product's monthly cost on top of the piece of paper. Let's say the product's monthly payment was two hundred dollars.) Then the sales manager starts itemizing the customer's monthly expenses: house payments, car payments, insurance payments, medical and electricity bills, etc.

When the total monthly expenses are lined up, and the secret two hundred dollars is included without the customer's knowledge, the master sales manager should say, "Mr. Customer, in total your monthly costs are around three thousand dollars; is that pretty close?" Remember, the customer wants the sales manager to think the three-thousand figure is accurate, so that the sales manager can see for himself that the customer can't afford another monthly payment on top of that three thousand dollars. After the customer agrees that this figure is pretty close to his monthly obligations, the master sales manager should say, "Mr. Customer, do you think we could add another two-hundred-dollar payment to this three-thousand monthly outlay?" At this point, the customer will think that he's off the hook and will say with conviction, "No way! I told you I can't afford the product. I'm strapped right now, as you can see."

This is when the master sales manager pulls the plug. He says to the customer, "Well, Mr. Customer, congratulations. You *can* afford this product. You see, I've already included the two-hundred-dollar payment in your three-thousand-dollar-a-month budget—so welcome to the club." The master sales manager should immediately turn the piece of paper around so the customer can see the expense list himself. At the same time, he should stick out his hand for a handshake agreement. The customer will come unglued. He'll have a blank look on his face—because he knows his ploy has been exposed. There is nowhere for him to go except to sign the contract, or to start scrambling for another reason not to buy.

The customer has just stated that he couldn't take on two hundred dollars more than the monthly figure they arrived at, thereby admitting that he could carry the hidden two hundred already figured in. The customer is completely taken off guard, and will probably admit that he could buy it after all. Instead of a triumphant "I told you so," the sales manager should start calmly writing up the purchase agreement at once, acting like the sale is a done deal.

This "T.O." close will work every time, if the situation is right. Don't forget, the customer has to *want* the product for this close to work. But work it does. It will take some practice to get this close down smoothly, but once it's mastered, sales will go up overnight. This powerful "T.O." close always gets the customer's attention.

CHAPTER 6

Saving Cancellations and Keeping the Sales Process on Track: How the Master Sales Manager Ties Up the Loose Ends of the Sales Operation

Now that the sales closers have successfully done their jobs and their company's sales volume is growing daily, there will always be a percentage of customers who want to cancel their sales contracts. It's just part of the selling profession. This is the time when the master sales manager can once again come to the rescue to retain that fickle customer and save the sale.

THE TEN MAJOR REASONS CUSTOMERS CANCEL

Following you will find a list of the ten major reasons why customers cancel their sales contracts, and what is the best way for a master sales manager to deal with each situation.

1. Simple Buyer's Remorse

This is when a customer simply gets cold feet. He starts to have second and third thoughts on every little thing about the product, right after he signs the sales contract. The real reason customers have buyer's remorse isn't the product, or the sales closer, or the sales manager—it's the customer himself. He lacks confidence in himself, and can't stand by his own purchasing commitment. In other words, the customer has scared himself by signing the sales contract and making a firm pledge. The reneger probably has a history of fearing commitment, as their ex-girlfriends or former boyfriends could confirm. This person doesn't need a better salesman as much as a better psychiatrist.

Remember that basic buyer's remorse is a phenomenon that happens to the weaker customers. They are the ones who get caught up in the sales closer's powerful enthusiasm, and in an uncharacteristic fit of energy and initiative, follow up the sales presentation with a purchase. Then, after the sales closer has left them and they don't have a "cheerleader" to keep them enthused, they crawl back into the shell of their normally diffident self and want to cancel.

2. Found a Better Deal

Another straightforward reason for a customer cancellation involves the customer finding a better price at another location. Again, there is no blame to be felt. The curious customer, after inking a deal, happens upon the same product for a more reasonable price, with a better guarantee, a better "extra," or rebate thrown in. This is all the excuse that some customers need to justify an immediate cancellation of their signed contract.

Saving some money at another outlet is all too often worth more than keeping one's word in today's world. Lest we think that the business world is populated with scheming customers victimizing innocent closers, it was probably the competing salesman with the better deal who showed the customer just how to cancel out on his first contract.

To keep this customer, you must cut your profit margin by lowering your price, or adding a "special extra," to make your product more desirable than your competitors'.

3. Lack of Funds

It's not uncommon at all for the customer to get home after purchasing that pool, car, or condominium; appraise his expenses, and realize that he simply can't afford the product after all. This customer most likely got caught up in the sales closer's enthusiasm, and signed that sales contract at a moment when his desire for the product exceeded his financial capabilities.

This is more likely to happen when a professional sales office employs a lot of super sales closers. In fact, the sales closers who don't get any cancellations for this legitimate reason are not doing their jobs.

4. Personal Problems

Soon after a customer buys or signs to purchase your product, he could find himself in some unpredictable situation that suddenly throws him into a financial bind. With the medical emergency, or uncovered damages he just experienced, he really can't honor the sales contract. When this happens, the customer will invariably cancel his purchase commitment.

The closer may first want to try to rearrange the payment schedule at such a time, but the customer who is reeling from a divorce, death in the family, etc., is usually in no state of mind to negotiate. To them the world has changed, and anything they signed a few days, or weeks, earlier seems a world away. The sales person who shows genuine concern, instead of irritation, may eventually win the customer back after he or she has recovered from the unexpected setback.

5. Lack of Understanding

Sometimes a customer seems to understand the general meaning of the document he is signing, but he doesn't fully grasp the finer details. He gets home and rereads the contract without the distractions of the closer and sales office, and lo and behold, he discovers that the affidavit doesn't state what he expected it to. The customer panics, and telephones the sales office to cancel.

Remember, reviewing the sales contract at the closing table is the responsibility of the master sales closer (or master sales manager). Sales closers, however, often hate to go over contracts in detail. Closers aren't supposed to have the temperament of lawyers, so one can't really blame them for skimming over the contract, and only stressing the good points, hoping that the customer puts away his signed contract and forgets about it.

NOTE: *"Buyer beware" is the customer's credo, but the closer or manager who glosses over contracts is courting customer cancellations.*

6. The Customer Feels Cheated

Many customers cancel their sales contracts if they feel that they were cheated in some way. They might see a negative news bulletin on television, or read about a recall in the papers, regarding the product they just purchased; maybe they feel that the sales closer flatly lied to them about the product and its performance. A customer could also feel that he paid too much for the product, given its quality. Don't argue with him. Refund his money.

It does not matter whether or not you feel the client is justified; remember, the customer is always right. Quietly, and quickly, refunding monies will avoid lawsuits or negative publicity that could be far more costly.

7. Belief Is Eroded

There are times when a cancelling customer has already made a few payments, and has owned the product for weeks or months. The customer's belief in your copier machines, or direct mail service, has eroded after some time, and now you have to settle on a prorated return to avoid the same difficulties mentioned above.

This can really be infuriating, especially if the customer comes up with an unlikely reason for the cancellation, or if he seems to have a cavalier attitude toward his contractual obligations. But the thrashed pride of a frustrated closer is easier to remedy than a summons to appear in court.

8. Bad Product

No matter how much pride we have in our product and in our company's quality control, keep in mind that some of the best apples can have a worm inside. Some cancellations will legitimately be for a product that simply doesn't work. You sell a quality automobile, and, though you hate to admit it, you inadvertently sold one individual a lemon.

You know that the customer has every right to complain, get an exchange, or cancel his sales contract. The customer has every legal ground to stand on, and he wanted his hard-earned money backed by your company's product warranty or guarantee. Your lack of confrontation and your sincere apologies for what is (hopefully) a rare mishap in production might earn you that product exchange instead of an outright cancellation.

9. Friends' Advice

There are always those inquisitive, "know-it-all" friends and relatives of the customer who want to throw in their two cents' worth of advice regarding the product just purchased. If these wonderful folks can't have the product themselves, they try to make the people who bought it miserable and suspicious. The really scary thing about these (so-called) friends' advice is that many customers actually believe their "folk wisdom" about homes at the bottoms of hills, those ugly rumors about the family background of the car dealer, or that televisions of this make have blown up and killed people.

Try to sound reassuring, even saying something nice about this obnoxious "friend." If the "my friend says" keeps coming back, however, you know the customer is not thinking for himself.

10. No Real Reason

Here we have a customer who doesn't know why he wants out—or at least he won't say why. It could be one of the reasons above, or he may be too embarrassed to admit that he can't swing the financing. This kind of customer tends to be very stubborn, even if you never get anything out of him other than the noncommittal "It didn't feel right."

Remember that a customer will always rationalize his actions rather than face the truth. The real reason for revoking a contract is always more difficult for the customer to accept, and only the master sales managers can discern what that motivation might be.

THE SALES MANAGER'S REACTION TO CANCELLATIONS

The master sales manager has distinctly different reactions to this situation—one as a professional, the other as a human being.

Professionally

When a master sales manager first finds out that a customer wants to cancel his sales contract, he's naturally going to be upset. The master sales manager, however, has a responsibility to everyone in his sales office to be the unshakable, exemplary leader, a person who doesn't come all unglued when things go badly.

The master sales manager knows that when a customer wants to cancel, it's either going to be his fault, his sales closer's, or the fault of the customer. The first step is to discreetly call the sales closer of the reneging customer into his office in order to discover any clues as to why the customer wants to cancel his contract. If the closer can't come up with a motive, then the master sales manager must decide if he wants to call the customer and try to save the sale, or if he should let the sales closer make the attempt. This decision basically depends on which of the two had the best rapport going with the problem customer.

The master sales manager also knows that time is of the essence, but good judgment also must be applied; some customers need to be appealed to right away, while others must be simply chalked up as losses, and referred to the refund desk.

Before the master sales manager talks to the problem customer, he wipes away any traces of disappointment, anger, or frustration, and adopts an air of sincere concern, care, and friendly warmth. Remember, you can attract a lot more bees with honey than you can with vinegar.

Now, the fastest way to communicate with the problem customer is by telephone. After the initial contact has been made with the problem customer, the manager must lure the client back to the office to regain the home court advantage. The master sales manager will disarm the customer with a warm "good loser" attitude, letting the customer think that he has won, and that he can easily get out of the purchase with a little paperwork. The master sales manager explains to the customer that this paperwork involves coming back to the sales office with the contract, and signing a document stating that the sale has been legally voided.

The customer may have rolled up his sleeves for a fight, and is now put off balance by this flood of sweetness and compliance. The customer does not realize that coming face to face with a master sales manager will make it a lot tougher for him to back out of his earlier commitment than a brief exchange on the phone or through the mail. When the problem customer arrives at the sales office, he is not ready for a fight and any weaker excuses for cancelling are likely to be overcome. The manager should not jump right into his contract-saving approach, but should first greet the customer with a warm and friendly attitude that melts away any antagonism. In a congenial atmosphere like this, it's very hard for the problem customer to remain frosty and uncooperative. His contractual problem may well disappear before very long.

Privately

Just how does a master sales manager feel deep inside about a customer who bought the product and then wants to cancel? Well, a manager wants to go up to that customer and make him literally eat that sales contract!

Hostility is undeniable; it is due to all of the time, effort, and negotiation that went to get that customer signed up in the first place. The good feelings everyone got basking in the glow of a completed sale (mission accomplished) has now soured and turned bitter.

The master sales manager will get it all out of his system and face that Indian giver with understanding, trying sincerely to walk a mile in the customer's moccasins. He knows he must attempt (in a reassuring manner) to talk with the customer face to face (if at all possible), and resell him on the product. He finds that in many cases a customer will honor the sales contract if someone takes the time to patiently listen to the customer's problem.

Again, anger or self-righteousness will only reinforce the customer's resolve. But throw a little love and understanding into the equation, and watch that resolve dissolve.

HOW A MASTER SALES MANAGER SAVES CANCELLATIONS

Getting the buyer back into the showroom is a master sales manager's major concern when he is trying to save a cancellation. Once he's got the customer in his domain, one or more of these ten methods will help you re-clinch what once seemed like a steadfast deal.

1. Simple Buyer's Remorse

The customer with buyer's remorse doubts his own actions. The master sales manager must build back the customer's confidence in the product. The master manager should convince this Doubting Thomas that he had made an honest and intelligent purchase.

At the same time, this weaker customer is just the one to tell that a deal is a deal, explaining that having second thoughts doesn't automatically erase a legal and binding contract. The master sales manager can use friendly persuasion or he can use the powerful weapon of "shame" to rein this problem customer in.

The master manager could say to the problem customer, "Mr. Customer, you and I are partners in this sales contract, and I'm going to do everything that I told you I was going to do. Now, I likewise expect you to hold up your end of our deal." (A small concession, like an extension of payment schedule, would go a long way at this point.)

2. Found a Better Deal

The customer who wants to cancel his sales contract because he's found a better product, or a better price, gives the master sales manager only two basic options:

1. The first, and the best, option is to match the competitor's price (once it has been confirmed as legitimate).
2. If the customer still wants out, the master sales manager must weigh the economic options. Would the company lose more from the loss of this sale than it would cost to take legal action? If taking the customer to court is economically feasible, then it's time to remind him that a court case might be necessary. Most likely, the customer will see that abusing his contractual agreement will end up costing him much more than it might save him.

3. Lack of Funds

Customers often cancel when they go over their budget at home and find out that they really can't afford to make the monthly payments, or live up to the conditions of the sales contract. The master sales manager must remember that the customer genuinely wanted to purchase the product in the first place, and the obstacle is purely monetary. Knowing this, the master sales manager should have a friendly heart-to-heart talk with this customer, and explain to him that he was once in the very same financial position.

The master manager should make the customer feel that his satisfaction is more desirable than his money, and generously help the customer work out a budget plan that will comfortably allow the customer to keep the product and not cancel the sale. The creative master manager should offer the customer better terms for referring new customers to his sales office, and should offer advice on loans, etc. Cancelling out on a legal sales contract is bad for one's credit rating, it should be added.

4. Personal Problems

The customer with a legitimate personal crisis needs a genuine friend. The master sales manager should sit down in private and listen with respect and empathy to the customer's dilemma. The master manager should then try to work around the problem to make it possible for the customer to keep the product without having to renege.

The sincere customer, in difficult circumstances, should never be strong-armed. If there is no way to work out a solution, then the master manager should refund the customer's money immediately and remain on friendly terms. The bonds of loyalty will pay off in the long run.

5. Lack of Understanding

In a situation where the customer didn't comprehend the entire sales contract, or some crucial details, it is up to the master sales manager to resell the product with complete clarity. The customer did want the product, so he warrants the extra time and effort to smooth over rough spots and renegotiate a deal.

Any intimidation with this customer will only backfire. He'll then be convinced that the company was out to get him with all the confusing fine print.

6. Felt Cheated

The customer who feels cheated or swindled is sure as heck going to cancel. In fact, he'll probably call his lawyer or the attorney general if he's got half a legitimate claim. In this kind of explosive situation the master sales manager should try to talk to this problem customer before he gets professional help. He must find out exactly what the problem customer is upset about, and immediately try to calm him down. The master sales manager must always avoid a scandal for his sales company by an immediate refund or product replacement.

7. Belief Was Eroded

The master sales manager must energetically resell the problem customer who no longer belives that the product will make his life better. This kind of problem customer has forgotten how excited and happy he was when he bought the product, and needs a booster shot from the master manager in an intense, intimate meeting. The manager can even try to sell him on an upgraded product. If he doesn't succeed, at least the customer feels as though he smartly avoided the more expensive model that he didn't really need.

8. Bad Product

When a customer wants to cancel his sales contract due to a bad product, the master sales manager should immediately explain to the customer how rarely something like this happens. He apologizes at once, offering the customer a brand new product and stressing that any future problems should be reported straight to him. The alternative could be the six o'clock news team knocking on the manager's door with TV cameras rolling.

9. Friends' Advice

When faced with a customer who wants to cancel his sales contract because his friends and relatives have dissuaded him, the master sales manager should point out (without ridiculing the friends or relatives) that his friends haven't been given the opportunity to hear a full sales presentation explaining the details of the product, so how could his friends possibly know how this product will benefit the customer's life.

The master manager must explain to the customer, that because he is more informed than his friends, he is therefore the authority on the subject—not his friends. This fellow needs self-confidence, so it must be pumped into him. Any problems that his buddy or cousin may have had with a similar refrigerator or condo is a separate case altogether, one which the manager can cordially invite the interloper to come in and discuss.

If these tactics fail, begin some mild intimidation with the line, "I presume your cousin is a lawyer who is aware of the implications of your not honoring this contract."

10. No Real Reason

Some customers do not admit to you or to themselves just why they want out of their sales contract. To dig down to this motive the master sales manager must gain the customer's trust with a friendly, caring talk about bonding subjects like hobbies, sports, travel, or family. This problem customer needs attention and reassurance. He wants the sales manager to hold his hand and tell him (in an authoritative manner) that he made a smart buying decision.

The truth can be smoked out, if the master manager takes some time with this problem customer and shows some T.L.C. This customer will not likely cancel once he's taken the first step of articulating his problem.

Note that, here, T.L.C. means "Taking the Lead and Control" as well as "Tender Loving Care."

TWENTY IMPORTANT TIPS ABOUT RENEGING CUSTOMERS

1. Buyers Are Liars

Problem customers will lie all day long to a master sales manager to try and snake their way out of their sales contract. They'll lie about:

  a. *What their sales closer told them*
  b. *What they did not understand about certain clauses in the sales contract*
  c. *The product not working right, or not being exactly what it's advertised to be*
  d. *What the guarantee states*
  e. *Signing the sales contract under the duress of a hard sell*

Problem customers will stay up all night scheming elaborate plans to get out of the sales contract. Believe it or not, a real problem customer can lie better and more professionally than many sales closers.

2. The "Notary Save"

Master sales managers should use the following bit of "preventive medicine" to protect them from future cancellations. After the customer has signed his sales contract and all the important paperwork has been handed back to him in a folder, the sales manager should hand him a simple (but official looking) card to sign before he leaves the office. On this card should be a typed description of the product, the date of purchase, and any serial numbers, measurements, etc. After the customer has signed this "official" card, the sales manager should immediately have one of his office personnel notarize it or stamp a seal on it in plain view of the customer.

The master manager should explain to the customer that this card is being filed away in a safe place for future reference. Should the customer later want to cancel his contract, the sales manager need only mention that notarized card that went into the company's computerized files with all of the customer and purchase information. The customer sees that tearing up his contract is not so simple, and that his previous purchasing commitment had many serious implications. Rather than upsetting all these official files, many a customer will waiver in his resolve to back out and will be more susceptible to a master sales manager's reselling efforts.

3. The Shoulder-Chip Removal

No matter how tough, how professional, or how stubborn the problem customer acts when he comes into the master manager's sales office to cancel his sales contract, he's still downright intimidated. The customer knows that the company is unhappy with him, and he doesn't know how he is going to be received. He's in "enemy" territory, so he's often feeling very defensive.

That big chip on the customer's shoulder will be smoothly removed by the master sales manager who treats him with unexpected warmth and understanding. Once the threatening atmosphere has melted into a spirit of cooperation, the master sales manager takes control, finds a solution, and saves the cancellation.

4. Keep Control

No matter what happens at this volatile time when a cancellation hangs in the balance, a master sales manager must keep all situations from getting out of hand. In a flash of anger the customer might even let fly some angry or vulgar language that would mean "fighting words" in another situation. The master manager must be courageous enough to stay calm, diffuse the anger with sensitivity and good humor, and stand firm—even if he thinks his company's policy is in the wrong.

Sometimes, a master sales manager can confide in a customer with a grievance that he has a legitimate beef, and that the company policy needs to be amended. The master sales manager should thank the customer for helping to bring up this flaw that will be addressed at the next meeting. Explain how you must execute the company's policy in the meantime, despite your personal regrets. The customer will be impressed with this kind of integrity and loyalty, and the cancellation might be dropped in the bargain.

5. Don't Apologize for the Product

When a problem customer is complaining to the master sales manager about a specific, defective product, he should make sure that his apology never sounds like a general apology for the entire company's products.

6. Customers Want to Believe

Believe it or not, most problem customers don't want to cancel. They honestly believe that they made a sound buying decision when they first bought the product. They do want the master sales manager to work things out for them and to restore that belief.

7. Don't Solve Two Customers' Problems Together

If a master sales manager has two unrelated problem customers that both want to cancel their sales contracts at the same time, he had better keep the two of them away from each other. The duo are only going to unite in their anger, feeding each other new complaints, and disrupting the whole sales office.

8. Husband and Wife Accuse Each Other

When the master sales manager is facing a husband and wife who argue with each other in front of him, blaming each other for making the purchase, the master manager has to first get the couple settled down before continuing on to try to save the sale.

9. After the Save, Shut Up

Right after a save, don't say anything else about the product. At this point, all you could do is jeopardize the save. Any talk should be happy chatter that is a distraction from the matter at hand.

10. After Six Payments

The sales manager must be concerned with the first seventy-two hours, the length of time legally given to customers to consider a sale. This seventy-two hour time frame particularly applies to real estate transactions, although other products have similar consumer protection plans. Remember the rule "Three days shaky, three months good, and six months solid." After six monthly payments you have everything on your side in the battle to save the sale.

11. Tell Third-Party Stories

An easy way to relax a problem customer is to tell a third-party story. Telling him about someone else who had the exact same problem a while ago and who got everything solved satisfactorily will go a long way toward putting a customer at ease and saving the sale.

12. Don't Hide Important Information

The master sales manager can never hide any kind of contract or product information from the customer; it is a potential time bomb just waiting to go off when the customer comes across the detail later on.

It's also against the law to withhold significant details that affect the customer's decision.

13. Let the Customer Cancel

If a sales manager ever finds himself begging for that save or working too hard with someone whose problem lies within his psychological being—he must stop! FORGET THE SALE! The manager's integrity and sanity is more important. Go on to your next triumph, and let this little setback fade into insignificance.

14. Use Intimidation

The manager should not hesitate to use intimidation when a customer fails to honor his sales contract for no good reason. He can stop a no-win conversation by saying something like: "My next words to you, sir, will have to be said in a court of law."

15. Don't Hide

It is tempting to run and hide from a hostile, problem customer spied coming through the front door of the sales office. This temporary way out is not worth it. The master sales manager is the leader of the whole sales organization, and he cannot demoralize the troops with a retreat. It will cause him to lose the control he maintains over his sales force.

16. Who Carries the Contract?

When a couple or group comes in with a problem, who do you concentrate on? Find out who is carrying the contract; he or she is the lead pin to roll for.

17. Keep Problem Customers Isolated

When a problem customer comes into the sales office to cancel his contract, keep him isolated in a private room away from everyone else. He's too negatively charged to be walking around telling every potential customer he meets how badly he's been burned.

If a master sales manager sees one of his sales closers purposely avoiding one of his own problem customers, and carelessly letting that hostile customer roam around the sales office—it is grounds for firing.

18. Listen to the Customer's Problem

Many customers do not get to the heart of their difficulty right away. Hear them out, don't cut them short, and don't presume that you know their problem before it is fully articulated. You could waste more time, and lose more potential saves, with misdirected solutions to the wrong problem.

19. Solve the Customer's Problem

The professional manager will do everything to save the sale of a reasonable customer who simply needs to talk out his problem in full. Don't worry about time wasted on someone with a long sob story. Save their sale and they will refer you and your product to many a friend with that same propensity for long-winded speech.

20. Kindness Kills Rudeness

It's hard as heck to practice all the time, but kind words and empathy will diffuse and calm down an angry customer. Instead of retaliating with heat, tell him: "Mr. Customer, I know you're very upset, but I promise you, I'll fix the problem right now and make sure you're completely satisfied."

Now you are on the way to a save, rather than a black eye.

SPECIAL INSTANCE: FIRING A SALES CLOSER

It isn't a pleasant duty, but when someone on the team is spoiling the spirit of the whole force, he or she must be quickly and quietly dismissed.

Here are reasons for firing a closer:

> a. *Lying to the sales manager*
> b. *Lying to customers*
> c. *Cheating fellow sales closers*
> d. *Constant lateness at sales meetings*
> e. *Not cooperating in group activities*
> b. *Being overly negative*

How to Fire a Sales Closer

Firing an employee can often be more distressing to the culprit's colleagues than to the manager or closer on either end of the pink slip. Therefore, the firing should take place behind closed doors, where no scene can be created by an angry closer cleaning out his work area. To launch a preemptive strike against the rumor mongers, calmly announce at the next morning's meeting why Closer Calvin had to be "let go."

On-the-Spot Firing

There are two kinds of situations where the sales manager has no choice but to fire a sales closer right on the spot, in front of the entire sales office: *(1) if the closer comes in intoxicated and causes a disturbance, and (2) if the sales manager has to make a public example of the firing; i.e., firing a lying closer at a time when several customers have complained about double-talking salesmen.*

Probation

The manager retains the diplomatic option of putting a problem closer on probation, perhaps a thirty-day trial period, rather than executing an outright firing. A closer might warrant this second chance if he has a long record of solid behavior, if he expresses regret for his actions, or if that occasional sinner happens to be the best damn closer in the state.

SPECIAL NOTES TO REMEMBER CONCERNING PROBLEM SALES CLOSERS

Especially if a fired closer is a talented and ambitious individual, take precautions to prevent him from stealing away customers, and even closers. You might be his mentor, but an angry closer could end up your competitor. Always take this possibility into consideration before taking any drastic actions.

And remember:

1. They Don't Like Themselves

The master sales manager has to remember one important thing about a problem sales closer. He or she is a problem because he's not happy with himself. He's frustrated because he's not as successful as he thinks he should be at this point in his life, so he carries a big chip on his shoulder, always looking at the dark side of things and resenting others who are more successful than he is. This problem sales closer can be helped if he wants to face reality and put the blame for his current circumstance where it belong—on himself. But most problem sales closers can't face that sobering truth and have to blame others for their shortcomings. This, in turn, only creates more problems. Remember, the problem sales closer lives in a vicious, maddening circle, always running away from himself but never escaping himself.

2. They Will Try to Steal Customers

The master sales manager has to know as a cold-blooded fact that there are some sales closers who (after they get fired) will come back to their old sales office or use phone connections to try and steal customers and take them to their new sales job. These kinds of dishonorable sales closers do exist, and they will in fact (to get some kind of revenge) try to direct the master sales manager's customers somewhere else. The master sales manager has to be aware of this type of problem sales closer. He can protect himself by either not letting the fired closer back on his property or by keeping a close watch for any unusual activity concerning his customer-generating programs. Customers mean money, and a vengeful sales closer who has been fired knows this fact all too well.

3. Put Them in Charge

If a master sales manager really wants to stop a problem sales closer in his tracks, he should make him an assistant sales manager. Give him some responsibility. That will make the problem closer shut up for a while and stop griping—guaranteed. The problem sales closer now has to put up or shut up. After telling everyone in the sales office how good a job he would do if he were the manager, and how he would change this and that for the better, he now has to prove it. He can't just complain about it anymore. All the master sales manager has to do is sit back and wait to see if the problem closer accepts his responsibility, thus becoming a reliable sales manager, or if he simply blows the opportunity and self-destructs. This great tactic on the master sales manager's part works; he just has to remember to keep overall control.

4. They Will Try to Steal the Sales Team

Problem sales closers who are fired and really upset with the master sales manager will sometimes try to take all of their old closer buddies with them when they move to another job. For example, they'll call the sales office and talk to all of their old friends and tell them about the great new job that they just found, or they'll tell their "gumbas" that they just landed the position of sales manager at another location and they need help setting up a new sales force. The master sales manager has to be the solid rock of Gibraltar in times like these, never acting as if he is upset or worried about losing his sales team. When all the hoopla and dust settles, the good, rational sales closers will realize where their future lies and will stay loyal to their master sales manager—the one person who never got rattled or felt threatened throughout the crisis.

5. They Will Try to Disrupt Sales Production

Some problem sales closers feel that if *they* can't be successful, then *no one else* should be. It's because of this mean-spiritedness that many problem sales closers will go out of their way to disrupt sales or make normal sales procedures difficult for a sales manager. For instance, if a manager asks this kind of problem sales closer to do something for the sales office or sales team, then he'll only do it half-heartedly, without any enthusiasm or team spirit. Or if the sales manager tells this problem closer to entertain some other closer's customers (for some good reason), he will do or say nothing to inspire the customer towards a sale for someone else. This problem sales closer will walk around the sales office with a frown frozen on his face and jealous hatred in his heart for everyone (customers and sales closers alike). The new customers who see him begin to wonder, "What's wrong with this sales company, anyway?"

6. They Will Borrow Money from Everyone

The master sales manager can tell when a sales closer is in trouble if that closer keeps borrowing money from the other closers on the sales force and won't come to him (the master sales manager) for assistance. This sales closer is having serious money problems, and he's either too embarrassed to discuss them with the master sales manager or he's afraid that he'll lose his job if the manager knows his messed-up situation. Whatever the case, a sales closer like this is not good for a sales force. Not only will he be resented and talked about (causing petty gossip), but he won't be a strong and independent member of the sales team anymore. He'll wind up resenting those who resent him, thus generating a negative attitude that doesn't help him, his team, or his customers.

7. They Will Spread Rumors

No matter what the master sales manager tries to do to prevent it, he can't stop a problem sales closer from spreading harmful rumors about him. It has to be remembered that most problem sales closers are just downright jealous of the master sales manager, and they honestly think that they can do a better job than he is doing. So, they start spreading fictitious rumors to make him look bad. Now, this sounds so very childish, but it's a real problem that plagues today's professional sales world. The master sales manager's only great weapon against such harmful nonsense is to be true to his profession and himself, to stay above the mudslinging. He has to conduct himself in such a respectable way that the rumors prove to be exactly what they sound like—rumors. Problem sales closers are easy to come by; true master sales managers aren't.

8. They Will Talk Badly About the Product

Another thing problem sales closers tend to do when they're unhappy is talk badly about the product that they are trying to sell. The problem sales closer will get together with other sales closers after work, often in their favorite watering hole, and complain about what he thinks is wrong with the product, the sales company, and the master sales manager. He'll bad-mouth a lot of people and policies as well as their product line, all along wishing that he were the master sales manager—or at least successful at selling. He is upset because he hasn't accomplished more in life and he wants to blame that fact on everyone but himself.

9. They Will Go Behind the Master Sales Manager's Back

A problem sales closer who dislikes his master sales manager (for whatever reason) will not only try to make petty problems for him, but he'll also go to the sales manager's boss (the president of the company) and tell little lies or exaggerate some sales office incident—anything to make the sales manager look bad or incompetent. Now, nobody needs this kind of "little weasel" around. Not only is he hurting the master sales manager to some degree, but he's really hurting himself, lowering himself to dirty tactics that don't work anyway. The master sales manager can only protect himself from this type of libel by consistently acting the part of true professional. Without stooping to the same level as his problem closer by striking out in revenge, the master sales manager knows that the baseless lies and innuendos will simply evaporate in a short period of time.

10. Deep-Down, Problem Closers Want Help

No person is so bad that his good side doesn't peek through if just given a little time. Problem sales closers can turn it all around if they have someone who really believes in them and sees their good side. They desperately need someone to encourage them to do their best. Some simple, kind few words can and do change people's lives. But who is going to take the time to deliver a powerful but simple phrase of encouragement? It's the master sales manager, that's who.

CHAPTER 7

A Summary for Keeping the Sales Office "Professional"

Following is a twenty-point guide to keeping a sales office "professional." All points should be taken seriously to heart in order to secure that sales success you are so intently looking for, for your company and its product.

A TWENTY-POINT GUIDE

1. Take Continued Care of the Customers

If a sales company doesn't take good care of its customers, then it won't last twelve months. When the closers sell someone their product, their job is only half done. The other half involves their taking care of the customer *after the sale*, making sure the customer stays satisfied and not forgotten. Only a fly-by-night company can afford to sell its products and then abandon its customers. Customers, not great products, closers or managers, ultimately keep the sales company going—simply because they have the money. A professional sales office and/or company has to treat each and every customer as if its whole existence depended on them—because it's true.

2. Keep Good Records

The master sales manager has to keep good daily records on every bit of important business done in his sales office if he wants to be truly successful. He not only has to keep daily records on financial concerns (for tax purposes), but he also must keep up-to-date records showing overall sales results, sales closers' closing percentages, cancellation percentages, and any other data reflecting sales production. For the master manager to run his sales office professionally, he has got to know how his business stands every minute of every day. And only good, solid facts and figures, put down in comprehensive records, charts or printouts will let him know. In fact, it's from this very important information that the master sales manager draws up his future selling game plans and marketing ideas. Don't forget that General H. Norman Schwarzkopf or Coach Don Schula didn't roll forward to victory until they had studied all of the facts at their disposal. Only then, intelligently, did they develop a plan to win. The master sales manager has to learn to do the same thing.

3. Don't "Talk Bad" About the Competition

If a sales company expects to remain successful and professional, then it should never stoop to throwing put-downs or below-the-belt blows against the competition. Now, this isn't the easiest policy to keep—to say the least—but in the long run it's the only right thing to do. Just as dirty politics often backfires, the ones who sling mud in business competition can't keep their hands clean. After a while, customers remain loyal to the sales company that always tries to abide by honest business principles, and the public invariably gravitates toward sales companies that play it clean. No one comes out a winner when one sales company downgrades another. The customer is not impressed at all when a sales closer tells him how much better his company is than someone else's. Sure, the customer will listen to the sales closer or master sales manager, but deep down he will feel no respect for that negative person. Remember this twist on the age-old adage: If you can't say something good about the competition, then don't say anything at all.

4. Get Young People Working in the Office

For any sales company to survive and stay successful, it has to get new blood into its system. If a company depends only on the good old pros, or only on old, tricky methods and sales techniques that worked in the "good old days," then that sales company will die a slow, painful but well-deserved death. Bright young people have bright new sales ideas that fit the younger generation of consumers. And these wonderful talents have to be used if a company expects to stay competitive. Sure, the basics of selling will always remain the same, but the young rookie closers have new attitudes and new computer skills to help the customer. Young people today can think up imaginative advertising and marketing plans because they have been exposed to so much more information. Of course, the young prefessionals can learn many lessons from the older pros, but there are some special and wondrous gifts that belong only to the younger spirits—especially those intangibles like energy, boldness, and the sense of adventure.

5. Don't Tell All Your Secrets

Any sales company that expects to be around for a long time had better practice the basic business code of not revealing sensitive information to everyone. If personnel who don't need to know are privy to what is happening, or going to happen, concerning the private business affairs of the sales office or sales company, then that company's element of surprise is perhaps gone, its element of negotiation is compromised, and its element of future development and growth is in jeopardy. A successful sales campany should conduct its key business matters in private, with only the principals attending certain meetings behind closed doors. The business world is full of "copy cats" who will steal a successful company's ideas or pre-empt a rival's marketing campaign, so secrecy is vital when operating a competitive business. The San Francisco Forty-Niners don't open their strategy sessions and huddles to the press either.

6. *Develop and Improve the Product*

A sales company can't stay successful if it doesn't try to improve its selling methods and/or its product line. Even a company has a proven product that it doesn't want to tamper with, it should explore new advertising approaches or promotion techniques. The reason? So the product doesn't get stale in the public eye, get to be taken for granted and soon forgotten. A sales company knows that the public is very fickle, and the best way to keep the consumers interested in a product is to maintain their curiosity. As for improving a sales company's product, the main goal should be to make the product more convenient, more useful and more cost-effective for the customer. If a company accomplishes these realistic and fair goals, it will sell everything it produces.

7. *Don't Depend on Cash Flow*

There isn't a file cabinet in the world large enough to contain all of the names of sales companies that have gone broke due to cash flow problems. Every day, a number of companies fail because money that was supposed to come in didn't. Now, this kind of disaster could usually have been avoided, if the sales company had only planned for the unexpected. For instance, a sales company should put away so much money every month in a "buffer account" to keep the company going for at least four to six months without any new capital coming in. A sales company with such a "buffer account" or "contingency account" can conduct business with a lot more confidence. When a company has to constantly worry about money coming in on time, then that will be felt throughout the sales office.

8. Man the Phones

There should always be someone on phone duty to handle customers' calls. If the sales company can afford it, then there should be someone manning the phone twenty-four hours a day, even on weekends. It's very important for a customer to feel secure in the fact that if he needs any information or help with his product, there is a phone number and a live person to contact. Customer service is second only to new sales when it comes to a sales company's priorities, and having someone live on the phone to help customers is more impressive than any multi-million dollar ad campaign. Customers will return your consideration in kind with new customer referrals and more sales.

> NOTE: Don't use answering machines if at all possible; people like to talk to people when they need help, not machines. Develop a "hot line" with call forwarding to a home number, if necessary. Let the customer know you care.

9. Send Out Newsletters

If a sales campany can afford a bit of time, money and effort, then it should put out at least a monthly newsletter to let employees and customers know how things are going, and what's going to be happening in the future. Newsletters keep the customer interested and keep the company's name on the customer's mind. There is no better way to sell a pool, for example, than to have satisfied customers and their new purchase beaming from your newsletter's pages. A newsletter will pay for itself many times over as these little upbeat stories do wonders for public relations and customer referrals. Let a leading sales closer or a proud new condo owner know that he is a "media star"—at least for that month.

10. Work a Referral Program

Any sales company that doesn't have an aggressive, attractive referral program is dumb. There is no other way to put it. Referrals mean the difference between just getting along and doing great. If a company worked on its referral program half as much as it worked on getting new customers, that company's sales volume would increase by a third. Referral customers are fun to sell, wonderful to know and great for generating other referrals.

A sales company can get referrals the following ways:

a. Using a legal "bird-dogging" system.
b. Acquiring names for a new mailing list from old customers.
c. Using retired sales closers' customers' friends.
d. Having customer "in-home" parties— or having invitational sales company parties promoting customer and guest discount programs.

NOTE: *For a company to be truly successful with referrals, it has got to use more than a follow-up program with previous customers.*

11. Promote and Reward

The master sales manager knows for a fact that rewards will get the people who work for him—from office personnel to sales closers—to perform up to their highest capabilities. The rewards could be in the form of flowers, plaques, money, or verbal recognition. It doesn't really matter. What does matter is that these rewards have to be promptly given to the person who has done something exceptional for the whole sales office. For maximum incentive value there should be no delays in handing out these awards. People like to be acknowledged as soon as they have accomplished something, not months or weeks later, and this way the excitement and enthusiasm doesn't fade. All this positive energy will entice the award recipient—and his colleagues—to work even harder.

This also holds true for promotions. When someone in the sales office deserves a promotion, the master sales manager shouldn't wait for a formal, end-of-season ceremony. At the earliest opportunity, go ahead and make the promotion. It keeps everyone working toward that bigger desk, private office or whatever perk you come up with to pique their interest. Remember: Always keep excitement alive with more excitement.

12. Advertise

If a sales company doesn't advertise its product, it is treading water and waiting to drown. It simply takes money to make money, and there is no way to get around this fact. A company has to let the public know about its product. Whether it's through television, the print media, radio, leafleting, or outdoor advertising, folks have got to know about the product before they can buy it. The secret to successful advertising can be all summed up in seven little words: "Get the public's attention, and keep it." If a sales company can catch the imagination of the public through its initial advertising, and then continue steadily "bombarding" the public with the same basic message, with variations, then the public will start to associate your product with your name. Product loyalties will set in and you'll attract a share of customer business.

13. Protect Your People

The professional sales office is only as good as the people who work for it. Everyday, the master sales manager has to let everyone working for him know that they are genuinely appreciated and respected. Not only does everyone in the sales office need to feel the same winning spirit when at work, but they have to know that office spirit doesn't just die when the working day is over. The folks in the sales office need to feel that they are members of a close-knit family that will always rally 'round when times get bad. Sales office personnel need to know that they can depend on their master sales manager anytime, day or night, to vouch for them and come to their rescue if necessary. When all the people in the sales office feel this secure, this important, then the master sales manager can hand them any kind of job assignment and it will be completed.

14. Keep Up with the Competition

The master sales manager had better know his competition. One of the most disastrous things that can happen to a sales company is for its competition to suddenly come out with a similar but better product. When it's too late to react, all of its old customers and potential customers are doing business with the other fellow. There is no excuse for this kind of business blunder. Even if a company has to use industrial espionage to find out what the competition is up to, then it had better use it, because the results of not keeping on top of the competitor's product could be fatal. Free trade and competition is the name of the game, and the more competitive one sales company is with another, the better for the consumer. But any sales company that refuses to compete, and thinks that it can survive on its past reputation, is stupid. There are plenty of secure "old giants" that are now parking lots.

15. Learn from Past Mistakes

Any sales company that doesn't learn from its past mistakes is doomed. Everyday in a professional sales office there are going to be mistakes made—and that's only normal. It's then, from these mistakes, that the master sales manager and his staff should learn a positive lesson. If the same mistakes are made over and over again, it's time for the master sales manager to follow the baseball rule: "Three strikes and you're out!" If a costly slip-up has been made for the third time (after two previous warnings) by the very same person, that person should be fired. When the master sales manager enforces the "baseball rule" the entire sales office tends to keep its eye on the ball.

16. Keep the Sales Office Shipshape

After a successful selling season, the master sales manager can't stop to rest and let the sales office, along with the surrounding grounds, go to pot. He has to maintain the office and landscaping in the very same immaculate way he did on opening day.

The master sales manager also has to keep all of the office personnel looking, feeling, and acting sharp. The reason? Old customers will always bring in new customers, so the sales office should run like a top, every day of the year. Remember, in the eyes of every new customer the sales office and grounds are the very first things that they encounter. Next comes the sales office staff. If either one looks shabby or unready for business, it will leave a bad impression on any new or unexpected customer.

17. Go Get Advice

When the master sales manager doesn't know exactly how to deal with a certain problem or situation that develops in his sales office, then he should get outside help. It doesn't matter whether the problem is a legal one or a financial one: Outside professional advice should always be welcome. A manager could make the problem worse because he had no idea what he was really getting himself into. Outside advice costs money, true, but in the long run it will be worth every penny. Of course, whatever the master sales manager hears and learns only makes him that much smarter. So the next time a similar problem arises in his sales office, he'll know exactly how to handle it.

18. Ask the Children

Believe it or not, a lot of major corporations have executives who go around to different elementary schools all over the world to ask children between the ages of five and eight how they like their company's product and how they would improve on it. Now, these children don't understand the details about the product, of course, but they do come up with some fascinating answers that the executives do, in fact, take back to their home offices.

For example, one major corporation asked kids how they could improve on their computer design (outside aesthetics), and the kids told them to make the "buttons" larger and paint them in bright colors for easy identification. Well, the corporation people told their design engineers, who proceeded to do just that. When the newly designed computer did go on sale, it was a complete success.

19. Be Available

In the navy, the captain of a battleship is always available to his men for any kind of unforeseen circumstances. Well, the same thing holds true for a master sales manager. If he expects his sales force to run professionally and successfully, then he has to be available to his crew and stick around the sales office. True, a sales force can get along without the master sales manager for a week or two—but no longer. Even with good assistant sales managers, or great side-kick sale managers, the sales closers start to get undisciplined after two weeks without the head honcho. It's primarily the general renegade make-up of master sales closers that causes this predictable phenomenon. In any case, the master sales manager has to be around to lead his troops. To prove this point, how many football teams have been have been successful when their head coach was away from the game? The answer is: very, very few. The sales force not only needs its master sales manager's wisdom, but also his leadership, his enthusiasm, his energy, his soft shoulder, and his iron hand.

20. Have Fun

If the people who work in a sales office aren't having any fun, then that office is not going to be successful. The master sales manager knows that if his people are always worried and over-serious, they will automatically be unhappy. And a group of unhappy people can't spread enthusiasm to customers. There is a football saying from the great coach Frank Broyles of the University of Arkansas that can very easily apply to business: "Take pride in your work, prove yourself on every play, have dedication, and have a good time, and the score will take care of itself." This is the kind of attitude that needs to be kept alive in any professional sales office. People create more imagine more, develop more and perform more when a sense of fun and team spirit permeates the office. The master sales manager has a very real responsibility to make sure all of his people have the same attitude that great athletes have: that they are lucky to be getting paid for something that is this much fun!

CHAPTER 8

Conclusion

Now you have the power of knowledge. And you can achieve it all! By having read *More Art of Closing Any Deal*, you possess the skills you need to become a master sales person. Your head should be swirling with inspiration, your heart thumping with excitement. Take what you have learned and implement it...be productive, be righteous, and be successful. Make your dreams come true.

NOW YOU HAVE THE WISDOM

WHAT EXACTLY IS A MASTER SALES MANAGER, ANYWAY?

You should answer this now-familiar question in your mind, before reading a word further.

In the preface of *More Art of Closing Any Deal* we asked, "What exactly is a master sales manager?" Now, some two hundred pages later, you have the answer. You now know a master sales manager is someone who can handle any sales-related situation effectively and successfully, someone who maneuvers his way through all circumstances using control and courtesy, understanding, and love.

Control

Control is the key word for the master sales manager. When dealing with the sales department, customers, or the president of the company, the master sales manager is always in control; he speaks with his mind, not with his heart. His emotions never get in the way of a business transaction. A master manager always makes his decisions in the company's best interest, not his own.

The master sales manager behaves in a well-moderated manner. He is the epitome of the ideal business person; warm, yet professional; wise; well dressed; tolerant, within reason; an expert on his product line, and in sales techniques. A master sales manager's working environment compliments his personality: stylish, yet conservative, and well appointed. Characteristically, a master manager is just, fair, and honest with his people; he is a big brother to his sales team, a friend to the customers, a valued employee to the board of directors. Personality flaws never come to the fore when a master sales manager is in a business situation. They are left at home, in the garage. Once he is in the office, the master manager uses his control to hide any character foibles. Instead, he positively approaches each day, attempting to be the best manager of the best sales team in history. He makes the most out of any given day, benefiting in every situation.

The master manager strives for the best. He puts together a sales team of the finest sales professionals possible, and endeavors to make them better, as both individuals and salespeople. Having achieved the role of a master sales closer prior to his appointment as sales manager, he understands what prompts sales closers to perform at their peak.

Meetings

Meetings are a key to sales success, and the master manager holds frequent, yet varied, meetings to keep the sales team striving for ultimate success. The meeting situation is a particular predilection for a master sales manager, because it allows him to demonstrate his discipline and control to his sales staff. The meeting is the sounding board for his ideas, a time when the master manager is on display as an effective roll model. By implementing whatever tactics necessary, such as motivational sales meetings, inspirational contests and parties, or bonuses, and then complimenting the group effort by whatever individual attention might be required, the master manager encourages his team to produce above corporate projections.

To get his sales team to progress to where no team has gone before, the master sales manager makes sure his sales closers are expertly versed in the facts, figures, information and the benefits of the products. To keep his team inspired, the master manager fine tunes his closers' sales skills, and helps his salespeople set, and achieve, their goals. He is the match that sparks the flame of "self-igniting" leadership in the hearts of his sales closers.

Experience

The master sales manager is an expert. He can take over any sales situation and, by complementing the appropriate technique with the necessary warmth and affection, he can succeed nearly every time. This is because of his wisdom and charm. A master manager can read his customers, and know how each effectively needs to be sold. This skill makes him the master manager; he knows his market, and his astute knowledge gives him the upper hand on the selling floor.

More Control

Control. That word keeps popping up, time and time again. If there had to be a single world to describe a master sales manager, that word is CONTROL. A master manager can oversee any situation, and conclude it for his company's best interests. The master sales manager has control over himself; he can act how he chooses, when he chooses. Impertinent, or negative, words and actions are never displayed.

Having mastered this ultimate discipline in himself, the master sales manager can take his well-focused control and project it to those around them, helping to influence their actions and decisions.

Time

Control, like the other skills involved in master salesmanship, takes time to develop. Nobody is born the best, and those who excel work at it. The biggest commitment it takes to be successful at anything is time and effort. You will immediately notice the improvement of your sales skills from reading *More of the Art of Closing Any Deal*, but the real benefits will come in the long run when you master your technique. In our highly competitive society, nothing comes easily. Always a healthy mental investment must be made before you can reap the fruits of your rewards.

BEING A MASTER CLOSER AND A MASTER SALES MANAGER

Work at being a master sales manager and the master sales closer, and you will eventually achieve this ambition. Always tell yourself you can be the best! After all, someone is going to be the best, so it might as well be you. You can be a master sales manager. Make it a goal. Work towards it. When you reach this target, you will know it, and you will feel fantastic.

Hopefully, you have already experienced the elation a master salesperson feels when he closes a monster deal, and the exceptionally pleasing sensation that accompanies the commission check. It's like flying. Success yields elation, an emotion that is virtually unparalleled in daily society. Success also yields increased self-confidence, something we all need for a complete life.

When striving for this success, don't make the financial reward your primary motivation. Money is nice, but it does not make for a complete person. So, forget the money. You will never succeed at becoming a master closer unless you strive for the emotional goals success has to offer. Once you are doing what you want to be doing, the money will come automatically.

Future master sales managers, now take what you have learned in this book and go out and conquer your goals.

The only person in the world who will try to stop you is yourself.

Remember: You can only lead others if they believe in you and you can only get others to believe in you if you truly believe in yourself.

The End